# Get Ready for Cloud Computing

D1372252

# Other publications by Van Haren Publishing

Van Haren Publishing (VHP) specializes in titles on Best Practices, methods and standards within four domains:
- IT management
- Architecture (Enterprise and IT)
- Business management and
- Project management

Van Haren Publishing offers a wide collection of whitepapers, templates, free e-books, trainer material etc. in the **VHP Freezone**: freezone.vanharen.net

VHP is also publisher on behalf of leading organizations and companies:
ASLBiSL Foundation, CA, Centre Henri Tudor, Gaming Works, Getronics, IACCM, IAOP, IPMA-NL, ITSqc, NAF, Ngi, PMI-NL, PON, Quint, The Open Group, The Sox Institute

Topics are (per domain):

| IT (Service) Management / IT Governance | Architecture (Enterprise and IT) | Project/Programme/ Risk Management |
|---|---|---|
| ABC of ICT | Archimate® | A4-Projectmanagement |
| ASL | GEA® | ICB / NCB |
| BiSL | SOA | MINCE® |
| CATS | TOGAF™ | M_o_R® |
| CMMI | | MSP™ |
| CoBIT | **Business Management** | P3O |
| ISO 17799 | CMMI | *PMBOK® Guide* |
| ISO 27001 | Contract Management | PRINCE2™ |
| ISO 27002 | EFQM | |
| ISO/IEC 20000 | eSCM | |
| ISPL | ISA-95 | |
| IT Service CMM | ISO 9000 | |
| ITIL® V3 | ISO 9001:2000 | |
| ITSM | OPBOK | |
| MOF | Outsourcing | |
| MSF | SAP | |
| SABSA | SixSigma | |
| | SOX | |
| | SqEME® | |

For the latest information on VHP publications, visit our website: www.vanharen.net, or freezone.vanharen.net for free whitepapers, templates and e-books.

# Get Ready for Cloud Computing

A comprehensive guide to Virtualization and Cloud Computing

Fred van der Molen (Lead Author)

# Colophon

| | |
|---|---|
| TITLE: | Get ready for Cloud Computing |
| SUBTITLE: | A comprehensive guide to Virtualization and Cloud Computing |
| LEAD AUTHOR/EDITOR: | Fred van der Molen |
| CONCEPT DEVELOPMENT: | Peter Hanselman, Virtualization and Cloud Strategist |
| EDITORIAL CONTRIBUTIONS: | Adrian Offerman |
| REVIEW BOARD: | Hans Beers, IBM, The Netherlands<br>Eric S. Charlesworth, CISSP, Cisco Systems, Inc., USA<br>Derek Cockerton, HP, UK<br>Edward Newman, EMC Corporation, USA<br>Steve Peskin – Virtual Clarity, UK |
| TEXT EDITORS: | Colin Brace, Martien Schrama |
| PUBLISHER: | Van Haren Publishing, Zaltbommel, www.vanharen.net |
| ISBN: | 978 90 8753 640 4 |
| PRINT: | First edition, first impression, December 2010 |
| LAYOUT AND TYPESETTING: | Internals: Imaginist, Leuven; Cover: ITpreneurs, Rotterdam |
| COPYRIGHT: | © ITpreneurs / Van Haren Publishing, 2010 |

For any further enquiries about Van Haren Publishing, please send an e-mail to: info@vanharen.net

Although this publication has been composed with most care, neither Authors nor Editor nor Publisher can accept any liability for damage caused by possible errors and/or incompleteness in this publication.

# Foreword

Ever since I was a boy, I have been fascinated by clouds. I would look up into the sky over England, intrigued by the various shapes and sizes that foretold of good or inclement weather. As this was England, it was more often than not inclement.
With a little imagination, it was also possible to see faces, animals, cars and other shapes. Sometimes the clouds seemed so low you could almost touch them but they were of course always out of reach.

In many ways things have not changed as the meteorological clouds of my youth have transformed into the technological clouds of the 21$^{st}$ century. As someone passionate about technology, I find it amusing how the similarities between the two work as a metaphor for where we are today.
As a boy vision and creativity could turn any abstract cloud into a sensitive sheep or a wily wolf. As a CTO, I seek to combine that same vision and creativity to turn abstract technological clouds into concrete services and solutions that improve the life of our customers.

As clouds drift across the sky they mutate, altering their appearance so that new shapes reveal themselves. In the same way the cloud configurations which are emerging in the market are continually adapting and changing their shapes to provide new possibilities.. Even as the real clouds seemed deceptively within reach before, they were always beyond my grasp. Today, certain cloud technology often seems closer than it really is and solutions can still be tantalizingly past our reach.

The good news is that the technologies that underpin the **Cloud Promise** are evolving at a tremendous pace and new configurations of solutions are rapidly becoming reality. Of these developments, virtualization has probably had the most impact to date. As stimulating as the technologies themselves may be, the real excitement will come from the new operating models that envelop and empower the cloud solutions. They will provide the real key to unlocking new opportunities for our clients and society as a whole.

Just try to conjure up what the world could be like in ten years. Hundreds of cloud providers both broad and niche, offering their components, stacks, patterns and solutions to a global market through dynamic contracts and spot pricing. A cloud futures market with hedging may well be commonplace. Through this ongoing brokerage and arbitrage, many assets as we know them today might even cease to exist and become but liquid commodities.

In this book you will read about the State-of-the-Art as it is being created in the top technology companies and service organizations around the world. You will also catch a glimpse of things to come. This book is part of a significant investment by the major technology vendors and companies such as ING to get our people and our customers ready for the change ahead. This book is part of a larger project for in company trainings on virtualization and cloud computing including   a series of training courses with international certification as well as e-learning, videos and a business simulation.

I would like to thank the many people who have made this book and the additional educational offering possible. I believe it to be the most comprehensive vendor neutral but vendor rich view into the state and future of one of the most important developments this century. Special thanks go out to my colleagues at the Enterprise Cloud Leadership Council, Sean Kelly, Michael Harte and Eric Pulier for their leadership, inspiration and vision.

My admiration also for Peter Hanselman and Rosanne Poolen who worked tirelessly within ING to bring this project to fruition and my Chief of Staff, Alan Nance for his vision in putting together the overall concept.

I believe that the great expectations inherent in the Cloud Promise can be achieved. Success will depend on how we combine vision and creativity with the technology available. This will be a stimulating journey that may well entail navigating a few sensitive sheep and wily wolves along the way. In that respect nothing has changed since I gazed into the sky as a boy.

**Tony Kerrison,** Head of Infrastructure Services, ING

# Acknowledgments

We are very grateful to various people for helping us get this publication done in record time.

Our first thanks goes to several IT leaders at ING who provided us the motivation and support to author this publication, including Tony Kerrison and Alan Nance. The fact that we received abundant access to experts and information within ING around the large-scale adoption of Virtualization/Cloud Computing technologies gave us various insights into the experiences of a large user organization. These will certainly benefit other organizations undertaking the journey to adopt the cloud computing in the coming years.

Next we would like to thank the review board, which worked diligently under very tight deadlines to review the content. The review board included Hans Beers from IBM, Eric S. Charlesworth from Cisco Systems, Derek Cockerton, from HP, Edward Newman from EMC Corporation, Steve Peskin from Virtual Clarity and Arjan Woertman from ITpreneurs. Many of these organizations further shared content, insights and experiences in the form of white papers, case studies, articles and other documents as inputs for this publication.

We would also like to thank Nic Barnes and Danny O'Connor (ING), Ton van den Berg (T-Systems), Glenn Brouwer (IBM), Derek Cockerton (HP), Ton Hofhuis (VMware), Ed Houweling (Microsoft), Paula Laughlin (EMC), Martien Ouwens (Oracle), JP Van Steerteghem and Brian Gracely (Cisco) for their contributions.

A very special thanks is also due to Fred van der Molen and Peter Hanselman who took on the challenging role of producing this unique publication in record time.

Finally, we are also thankful to the people at ITpreneurs and Van Haren Publishing whose cooperation and teamwork made this publication a reality.

Sukhbir Jasuja
CEO, ITpreneurs

## How This Book Is Organized

Have you heard a lot about cloud computing lately? Are you wondering what the impact of the cloud will be on your organization? Then this book is for you. It isn't intended to be an exhaustive technical manual on virtualization and cloud computing strategies. In fact, we try to avoid IT jargon whenever possible. In clear, concise language, *Get Ready for Cloud Computing* will help you understand the basic underlying principles of cloud computing and guide you in making a business case for implementing the cloud in your organization.

In the first two chapters, we offer insights into the history and visions behind cloud computing concepts. These chapters provide an overview of the cloud model and the forms it is taking. We also explore how organizations can profit from cloud-enabling technologies and how they can incorporate them in their own IT-infrastructure.

Chapter 3 deals with Virtualization. In this chapter, we take a look under the hood of the cloud. This section is a bit more technical, but you will find it worth while, as the concept of virtualization is really at the heart of the cloud.

Part II of the book offers in-depth articles from industry experts who are working with leading IT vendors in the field of cloud computing.

In Part III, we share a number of interesting case stories, covering a broad range of virtualization and cloud related issues. Some of these stories were made available by vendors, others were researched by our editorial team.

As you will see, there are compelling reasons to get up to speed on this exciting and rapidly-evolving new dimension of the Internet. Reading *Get Ready for Cloud Computing* is the perfect start.

**Fred van der Molen (Editor/Leading Author)**

# Table of contents

Get Ready for Cloud Computing

# Part I
# An Introduction to Cloud Computing and Virtualization

# Understanding the Cloud

Fred van der Molen

# 1. Understanding the Cloud

## 1.1. Introduction

"You may recall the childhood story of Chicken Little being hit on the head by a falling acorn", is the surprising start of an article about cloud computing by HP's Keith Jahn. In 'Making the Cloud Relevant' he memorizes the story about the seemingly life-or-death journey of a frantic hen who feels obliged to inform the king about her finding that the sky is falling down. Along the way Chicken Little gathers supporters. Later on the group runs into a fox who advices them to take a shortcut so they will arrive more quickly to the king. According to Jahn, there are two popular endings to this old story:

> ⊡ The animals are eaten by the fox and never see the king, espousing the age-old lesson of "do not believe everything you hear."

> ⊡ The king's hunting dogs intervene and dispatch the fox enabling the king to hear the story, teaching a lesson about courage and perseverance in pursuing goals.

What, if anything, does this story have to do with IT?
Jahn explores in the article a scenario that IT organizations could face in the not too distant future, brought about by the advent of the cloud phenomena - one that forces radical change or results in dire consequences for IT as we know it, and perhaps even removing the function altogether.

Although the metaphor is a bit limp, IT veterans probably have heard "the sky is falling" stories twice a decade. The IT sector is full of hypes. Both versions of the Chicken Little story have materialized. UNIX did not kill the mainframe; the thin client did not kill the PC; the year 2000 bug did not stop the world; the old economy survived the new one.
But once in a while there is indeed a real "inflection point", as Intel's former CEO Andy Grove put it: a moment in history in which the way of doing things fundamentally changes, mostly due to new technologies. Such a moment gives new players a chance to break into existing and divided markets. At the same time, it can be the beginning of the end for old companies which do not recognize the new and unexpected challenges.

> In 2003 Nicholas Carr wrote his bombshell book "Does IT Matter?"

The introduction of the PC was such a moment, and even more so the establishment of the World Wide Web. Most probably the introduction of the iPhone will turn out to be an inflection point as well. And now we have cloud computing, which will turn out to be yet another disruptive technology.
Cloud computing is the next stage of the Internet computing model, one in which business will consume services, not technologies. And these services will be ready to run, available outside the office walls, and be paid for on the basis of usage, just like water or electricity. As the cloud and services model matures, business will be able to solve old problems more inexpensively and rapidly. And what's more: they will be able to address new challenges that they were never able to address before.

Back in 2003, Nicholas Carr wrote his bombshell book "Does IT Matter?". Some of his predictions have come true already. The cloud will force business to change, and ever more, force IT providers and departments to change. This will not happen overnight. It will not be next year, or in a year or two, but more and more companies will have a real choice to source services wherever they like: inside the organization or from any provider, whether it be Google, IBM, Microsoft, Amazon, T-Systems or any other cloud vendor.

Cloud computing is driving a fundamental change, enabling IT managers to treat infrastructure as a common layer, on which they can provision services to users faster in a much more flexible and cost-effective way. From a technology point, the journey to the cloud is more an evolution than a revolution. It builds on decades of IT innovation and is hampered at the same time by decades of infrastructure and application development. And yes, there are legal, security, and compliance issues. But at the end of the day, the potential benefits of the cloud computing paradigm are too overwhelming to be ignored:

**Benefits cloud computing:**

- [>] Improved business agility

- [>] Reduced capital expenditure

- [>] Increased end-user productivity and collaboration

- [>] Reduced energy consumption

## 1.2.  A Brief History of Cloud Computing

Referring back to old mainframe-practices from the seventies, some IT veterans dismiss cloud computing as just 'time-sharing on the Internet'. That's a witty thought, but not even half the truth.

But yes, the cloud is not new. Existing technologies, such as grid computing, utility computing or adaptive computing, mark the infrastructure path leading to cloud computing; application service providing (ASP) signifies the growth towards the provision of programs. The cloud is the next stage in the evolution of the Internet. It provides the means through which everything from personal collaboration, computing power, storage to business processes is delivered to you as a service. Services like Gmail, YouTube or credit card validation are good examples; you get the service when you need it and wherever you are, provided of course you have an Internet connection.

By the way: the term "cloud" originated in the telecommunications world. Telecommunications networks and the Internet were visualized on technology diagrams as clouds, signifying areas where information was moving and being processed, without the average person needing to know exactly how that happens. And actually that's a still central feature of the cloud: the customer asks for and receives information without knowing where it resides or how the services in the cloud fulfill the request.

The history of cloud computing started in the nineties with the creation of the World Wide Web. With the Mosaic browser, Internet-based computing took off. From a business perspective, it brought us virtual shopping experiences and chain integration. The concept of e-business acquired a foothold in almost every company. As a valuable side-effect, consumers became acquainted with leading-edge technology while searching for information, doing online shopping, communicating with their friends and family, watching movies, or managing bank accounts. The seed of the cloud was sown.

The next generation of cloud services was driven by these consumer experiences: available 24/7, an intuitive user interface that didn't require training, and comprehensive self-services,

*Figure 1.1 - The evolution of Cloud Computing.*
*Source: 'Making the Cloud Relevant', HP White Paper*

| | Cloud 1<br>e-business | Cloud 2<br>IT as a Service | Cloud 3<br>Everything as a Service |
|---|---|---|---|
| **WHY**<br>forcing function | ▷ Internet-based supply chain integration and e-commerce | ▷ Consumerized Internet services<br>▷ Low-cost IT | ▷ Pervasive business and consumer service |
| **WHAT**<br>technology orientation | ▷ Web-based app design<br>▷ EAI and message bus integration<br>▷ Internet protocols<br>▷ 3-tier architecture | ▷ Web 2.0 and SOA app design<br>▷ Virtualization<br>▷ Cloud-based technology platforms | ▷ Data-oriented, context-aware services<br>▷ Vertical and horizontal ecosystems |
| **HOW**<br>IT organization design | ▷ Organized around technology domains<br>▷ Technology-centric | ▷ Organized around service supply chain<br>▷ Service-centric | ▷ Organized around value networks<br>▷ Service-centric |

| 1990 | 1995 | 2000 | 2005 | 2010 | 2015 | 2020 |
|---|---|---|---|---|---|---|

from opening a new bank account to booking a holiday trip. Technology evolved to create rich interactive web interfaces and service-to-service interaction. Welcome to Web 2.0! Interestingly, innovation in consumer-oriented services progressed far beyond business applications. Web 2.0 more or less forced its way into the enterprise on the backs of the employees. Cloud services like social networks and collaboration tools, for example, changed the way business people access and share information. At the same, time companies like Google and Amazon started offering their storage and computing capacity to business and consumers.

Today, most of the attention around cloud services in the enterprise is focused on these kind of techniques and sourcing alternatives for IT capabilities; it all comes down to IT as a service. Using standardized, highly virtualized infrastructure and applications, this new approach can drive higher degrees of automation and consolidation, thus reducing costs.

The evolution of cloud computing is now entering phase three: Everything as a Service. At the end of the day most of the enterprise infrastructure and applications will be sourced as services in an on-demand manner. This can be in a "public cloud" like Google or within the (control of the) organization as a so-called "private cloud".

## 1.3. Business Innovation

The cloud service orientation is also generating new ideas for business innovation. Companies are beginning to discover new sources of value in cloud services. First of all, the cloud can lead to cost and efficiency savings. Second, the cloud model can eliminate some of the constraints inherent to traditional architectures and service delivery models, for example in chain integration and collaboration.

Meanwhile, business people are attempting to further exploit the service orientation to remove complexity in their processes. The new generation of "digitally native" employees visualize new opportunities but feel "held hostage" by their IT department. This is adding stress to the already troubled relationship between IT departments and the rest of the organization.

While many companies are wrestling with the technology transitions required to move to Web 2.0, the volume of services in the commercial cloud marketplace is increasing and new web technologies are emerging.

> Cloud computing is a potential cost saver but does not always save money

Not surprisingly in today's economic climate, the desire to save money is present in all IT-discussions.

Cloud computing is a potential cost saver but does not always save money. It can drive costs up if it is used to replace on-premises work with an exact duplicate in the cloud. Knowing when to redesign is critical.

As we move beyond traditional computing paradigms, we enter an era where everything becomes a service: from software as a service to business processes as a service. This will inevitably change the way we think about running our businesses.

A New Era of Innovation

The IT industry has seen several paradigm shifts over the past four decades. Mainframe computing enabled businesses to automate manual processes and achieve growth not limited by the number of employees; the personal computing era empowered professionals to run their businesses based on individual data and applications. Then a decade of network computing and client/server-technology established a new level of information exchange

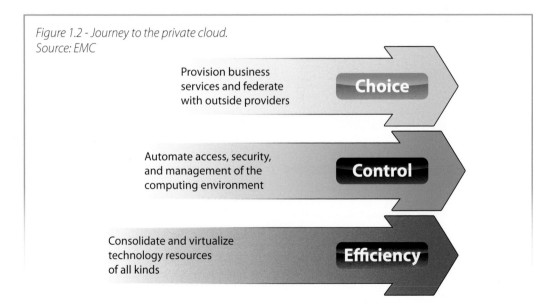

Figure 1.2 - Journey to the private cloud.
Source: EMC

Provision business services and federate with outside providers — **Choice**

Automate access, security, and management of the computing environment — **Control**

Consolidate and virtualize technology resources of all kinds — **Efficiency**

inside and between companies. According to Forrester Research, each of these revolutions brought with it new economies of scale. The cost-per-transaction, the cost of automating office and desktop processes, and finally the cost of network bandwidth fell quickly and enabled business users to apply ICT solutions more broadly to create business value. Forrester believes that cloud computing will help unleash the next wave of tech-enabled business innovation, which it calls Smart Computing.

The Forrester researchers (The Evolution Of Cloud Computing Markets, July 6, 2010) see three major market forces both enabling cloud computing as well as driving its adoption by users and service providers:

1. **IT Becomes Embedded in the Business**
   The Internet has already driven a gradual migration of functionality from applications designed for single departments or processes toward resources that are shared and interconnected. Offering IT resources as a paid service makes users aware of costs, unlike traditional measures such as the speed or volume of technology infrastructure. Buyers are more likely to judge technology investments in business terms, measuring technology value in terms of improved business outcomes. Forrester refers to this evolution as the shift from information technology to business technology.

2. **Shared Service Architectures Mature**
   The massive shift toward Internet-based shared IT resources reinforces the preference for one-to-many service architectures. Internal consolidation and virtualization of data centers is just the beginning. The quest for higher utilization of IT resources then leads users to try out shared platforms operated by external service providers, which have significantly higher levels of resource sharing and lower costs per unit.

3. **Technology Populism Spreads**
   As the overall population becomes more Internet-literate, consumers are using technology to manage and integrate their private and business lives. The rapid evolution of the personal cloud services and mobile digital devices raises business users' expectations for immediate, universal access and unlimited scale of technology resources.

> Forrester: cloud computing will help unleash the next wave of tech-enabled business innovation

According to Forrester, cloud computing has already had an impact on many of the segments of the $2.4 trillion worldwide spend by businesses and governments on ICT products and services. At the highest level, cloud computing changes how customers deploy software applications and middleware, it draws spending from portions of the outsourcing market, and it cannibalizes customer investment in hardware and data centers.

## 1.4. Is It a Cloud? Characteristics

Back to basics. Time for a reality check. We know the IT industry is good in generating hypes. Every vendor is talking about cloud this and cloud that. Some of them just seem to have replaced the word "Internet" for cloud or re-labeled everything as a cloud service. But what makes a cloud a cloud?

As we have seen in the three cloud diagram in Figure 1.1 cloud computing is still an evolving paradigm. For the moment, let's stick to the definition of the US-based National Institute of Standards and Technology (NIST).

Definition NIST:

> Cloud computing is a model for enabling convenient, on-demand network access to a shared pool of configurable computing resources (e.g., networks, servers, storage, applications, and services) that can be rapidly provisioned and released with minimal management effort or service provider interaction.

That's quite a mouthful. Essential is that the cloud is not defined as a set of technologies but rather a model for delivering, managing, and consuming information technology resources and services.

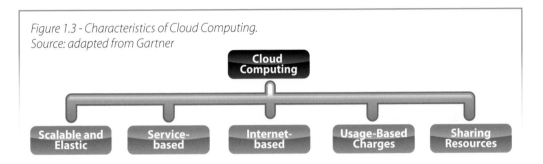

*Figure 1.3 - Characteristics of Cloud Computing.*
*Source: adapted from Gartner*

According to NIST, as well as others, the cloud model is composed of five essential characteristics, three models, and three service models. We will examine these one by one. First, the essential characteristics (we derive these from different sources, including NIST and Gartner):

## Scalable and Elastic

In a cloud world, a service provider can't anticipate the usage volumes or demands for services. It doesn't need to either. The service is always on (24x7), scalable, and flexible by design. The cloud is elastic like a rubber band. To the consumer, the available resources appear to be unlimited, and they can be accessed and purchased in any quantity at any time.

## Service-based

In a cloud world users can unilaterally provision an application, server time, storage or a business process, as a service. This can be done on-demand without requiring human interaction.

## Internet-based

And yes, this is an Internet World, so cloud services have standardized web services interfaces. These standards promote use by heterogeneous client platforms (e.g., PCs, thin clients, mobile phones, and PDAs).

## User-based Charges

Sorry, there is no free lunch, unless you would like to introduce an advertising-driven revenue model like Google inside your business. Cloud systems have a metering capability appropriate to the type of service (e.g., storage, processing, bandwidth, or active user accounts). Resource usage can be monitored, controlled, and reported. And yes: your cloud services provider sends you a bill, just like the power company.

**Sharing Resources**

Cloud services are multi-tenant, either at the hardware layer or software layer, but ideally at both. This means that a single instance of software, and the computer platform it runs on, serves multiple clients. There is a sense of location independence; the customer generally has no control or knowledge over the exact location of the provided resources but may be able to specify location at a higher level of abstraction (e.g., country, state, or data center). Sometimes this is needed for legal reasons.

## 1.5.   Cloud Delivery Models

When one says "cloud computing", people probably first think of services offered by well-known companies such as Amazon, Google, Facebook, Twitter, YouTube and Salesforce.com. This is the "public" cloud, where you can use resources for free, or rent computing and storage capacity, as well as a growing array of business applications and services. Making a division between the public, private and hybrid deployment model is a popular way of making a "slicing" into cloud computing.

### Public Cloud

A public cloud is made available over the Internet to the general public or a large industry group and is owned by an organization selling cloud services. These services are offered via the Internet in a standardized, self-service, and pay-per-use form. The public cloud is a mass-volume, highly standardized IT services market with low margins.
From a vendor perspective: the cloud provider is the vendor. Besides relative newcomers as Amazon, Google, and Salesforce, well-established Internet providers (Terremark, T-Systems) and traditional IT-vendors (IBM, HP, Microsoft, SAP, Cisco, EMC and Oracle) have entered this market.

### Private Cloud

A private cloud is operated solely for a given organization. It may be managed by the organization itself or a third party and may exist on premise or off premise. Aside from the underlying technology, an important difference between large-scale corporate data centers and private clouds is the governance model. In the cloud model "the business" really is the customer. The risk of fluctuating utilization is on the IT side rather than on the business side. A challenging new perspective for CIO's is that the IT department is not a cost center anymore; it is a service provider that is financed by contributions from the business units.
From a vendor perspective, the private cloud is essentially a market for licensed tools, hosting and consulting.

### Hybrid Cloud

The cloud infrastructure is a combination of private and public clouds that remain unique entities but are bound together by technology that enables data and application portability. It combines elements of public and private clouds, including any combination of providers and consumers, and may also contain multiple service layers.

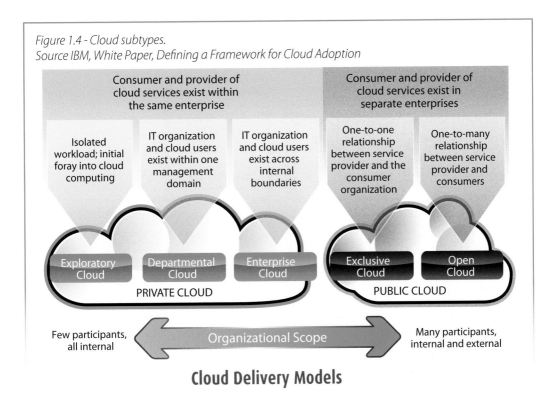

*Figure 1.4 - Cloud subtypes.*
*Source IBM, White Paper, Defining a Framework for Cloud Adoption*

**Cloud Delivery Models**

In cloud computing literature, one will find all kind of refinements, like the delivery model subtypes in Figure 1.4 from IBM. This figure shows a cloud computing adoption framework starting with an Exploratory Private Cloud at the left to an Open Public Cloud at the right. These distinctions are relevant for a more targeted discussion of roles and responsibilities for both the provider and the consumer of cloud services, but we will be tackling that in this introduction.

## 1.6. Cloud Service Models

Let's look now at the common types of service models.

### Infrastructure as a Service (IaaS)

These type of cloud services provide on-demand, pay-as-you-go access to computer resources, (servers, networking and storage). This also includes the delivery of operating systems and virtualization technology to manage. The customer is renting computing power rather than buying computers and software. This service is typically paid on a usage basis - for example, by the hour or gigabyte transferred - or as a fixed fee for a virtual device with an agreed-upon capacity and configuration.
These kind of services involve an straightforward Service Level Agreement (SLA), in terms of availability, capacity and performance. Examples of cloud infrastructure providers include Amazon Web Services, Terremark Infinistructure, Hosting.com and Savvis.

*Figure 1.5 - Service Models.*
*Source: NIST*

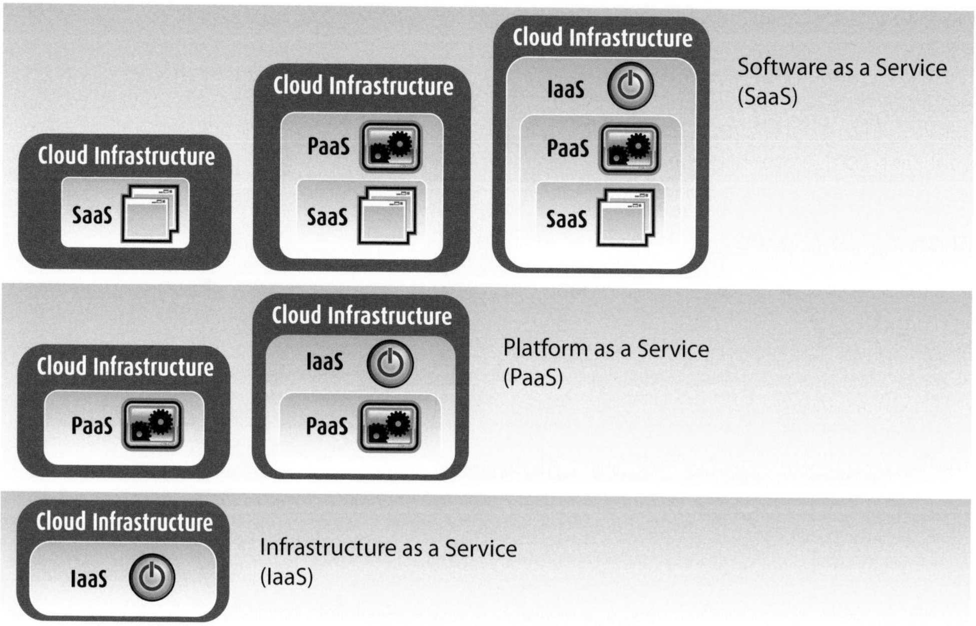

## Platform as a Service (PaaS)

These services deliver compute capability (infrastructure) that is typically aimed at developers or advanced IT users. The customer deploys applications created in house or acquired elsewhere using programming languages and tools supported by the provider. The customer does not manage or control the underlying cloud infrastructure (network, servers, operating systems, or storage), but has control over the deployed applications and possibly application-hosting environment. PaaS addresses the need to scale without upfront investments. A possible disadvantage is certain degree of vendor lock-in. There are proprietary elements in most platforms. Examples of PaaS are web servers, Force.com (the development environment for Salesforce.com) and the Google App Engine.

## Software as a Service (SaaS)

When we move up in the stack, the next layer is SaaS. The service provider offers the customer the ability to run predefined business applications that are hosted by the provider. SaaS has its roots in the nineties in hosting operations carried out by Application Service Providers (ASPs.) As a cloud service it comes with pay-per-use, self-service and dynamic scaling characteristics. SaaS-applications are already widespread. The applications are accessible from various client devices through a thin client interface such as a web browser (e.g., web-based email). The consumer does not manage or control the underlying cloud infrastructure including network, servers, operating systems, storage, or even individual application capabilities. Applications in this space include Salesforce.com, Microsoft SharePoint Online, IBM LotusLive, Expedia.com and Google Apps. Other major vendors like

SAP, Oracle and HP all have SaaS offerings as well.

The most obvious advantage in buying software as a service is that the customer does not have to buy any hardware or software. You can share information with external partners more easily without having security concerns. There are no upfront investments and the price is likely to be lower. Environments such as Facebook, YouTube, Google Apps, and others are all designed for massive scaling. As a customer you make advantage of the economy of scale of these providers. And what's more: the provider does all the heavy lifting in the data center. Biggest disadvantage is probably the limited configuration options. One should be aware of security and compliance issues as well.

## Business Process as a Service (BPaaS)

This service combines application cloud services and the shared services model in which a single organization delivers business services, such as purchasing, holiday booking, employee benefits management, help desk or procurement, to multiple internal or external consumers. This has its roots in the traditional outsourcing business, where complete business processes – such as IT maintenance – were turned over to external experts.

# How to Catch a Cloud?

Fred van der Molen

# 2. How To Catch A Cloud?

## 2.1. Business Drivers for Adopting Cloud Principles

A lot has been said already about the proclaimed benefits and business drivers for cloud computing. We will now investigate that in detail. Of course there are drawbacks and risks too. We will get to those later as well.

### Improved Business Agility

'Agility' has become a familiar buzzword at CIO-seminars lately. And indeed, cloud computing services make it easy to add new users, new capabilities or increase or decrease capacity. Flexibility and faster time-to-markets make a difference in an age when markets are evolving more and more rapidly. Not only do successful companies recognize market opportunities early but they are also able to respond to them quickly as well. Therefore, organization and business processes should be geared towards agility and flexibility.

Using a cloud computing model, IT staff can meet changes in user loads quickly without having to invest and engineer for peak loads. Elasticity is a benefit when enterprises are growing, providing the opportunity to purchase capacity on the margin at predictable costs. And, equally as important, the cloud also provides the means to scale down a service cost-effectively and quickly when it is no longer needed or the demand diminishes.

> As cloud computing converts fixed costs into variable costs, it releases capital for investment in other areas

For example, your department wants to try out a new business application. Instead of embarking upon a decision-making trajectory of perhaps months in duration, you now can try out, develop, and even test a new application without first investing in hardware, software, and networking. This can have a very positive impact on innovation.

### Reduced Capital Expenditure (CAPEX)

With external clouds, you do not have to invest upfront in infrastructure. This enables enterprises to minimize capital expenditures and still increase functionality. As cloud computing converts fixed costs into variable costs, it releases capital for investment in other areas. Or, it can enhance the balance sheet strength of a company.

With cloud computing, you can consume new resources as a service, paying only for what you use. Clouds also enable IT departments to save money in the long run on hardware-investments, application implementation, maintenance and security costs. If your organization were to start from scratch, you could reach costs benefits with a private cloud infrastructure up to 45%, according to a study of vendor EMC. (Figure 2.1) IBM studies give about the same cost reduction figures, but the actual reductions an organization will achieve will of course vary depending on the starting situation.

Although a cloud scenario can drive costs up at first if used to replace on-premises work, hardware is perhaps the most obvious cost reduction factor. In the long run, cloud infrastructures, running multiple virtual systems per physical host, are cheaper. One should not however underestimate the complexity of the overall management of these virtualized

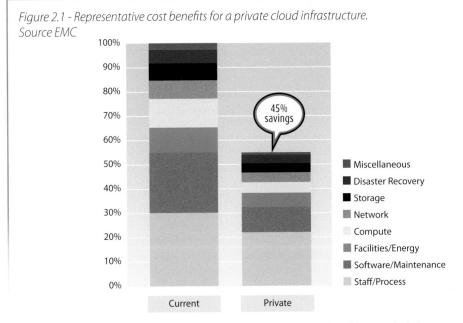

*Figure 2.1 - Representative cost benefits for a private cloud infrastructure. Source EMC*

environments. New virtualization-aware system management tools will be needed. Once these are deployed, however, cost savings are substantial. Computing power, storage and network components will be utilized far more efficiently; fewer administrators can manage a larger number of servers. Cost-reduction opportunities can be found in maintenance, system administration, facilities, energy consumption, and so on.

## Increased End-User Productivity and Collaboration

Cloud computing increases user productivity and collaboration. With a cloud solution users can access services regardless of location or device. And they can easily share information with colleagues or partners.

## Less Energy-Consumption

"Going Green" is a important focus for many enterprises. Clouds and virtualization enable organizations to reduce power consumption and space usage.

## Improved Reliability and Continuity

Maybe this should stay a secret, but cloud providers have less downtime than most companies with internal data centers. Cloud computing, private or public, can also cost-effectively provide redundancy sites, facilitating business continuity and disaster recovery scenarios. The virtualized and automatically managed environment of a (private) cloud infrastructure enables better compliance with information management and privacy regulations, more secure remote access to corporate information, and faster and more reliable backup and recovery of information systems.

## 2.2. Defining a Roadmap for Cloud Adoption

The public cloud consists of a fast-growing array of services offered by very large and relatively new players like Google and Amazon. The unit cost is low and the scale is enormous. A small business can source its entire IT-infrastructure and some or most of its business applications to the public cloud.

For startups, the public cloud is probably a no-brainer. However, for large and established organizations, with business-specific legacy applications and a lot of sensitive information, relying heavily on the public cloud might be infeasible and unwise. As Gartner Group explained in 2009, "For most IT services, cloud services do not exist, are not proven, do not meet service-level requirements, do not meet regulatory or legal requirements, are not secure enough, or all of the above." (Thomas J. Bittman, "Private Cloud Computing: The Steppingstone to the Cloud," June 2009)

By law, companies remain responsible for their data, but you may not know where your data is being stored (that alone can violate national laws) and how exactly it's being protected. All this will changeover time. Public cloud offerings are expanding and improving all the time, and it may be the best source already for selected (especially new) business applications and services. For example, many large enterprises have decided to use public cloud services for mail, collaboration, human resource management (HRM), education, and customer relationship management (CRM).

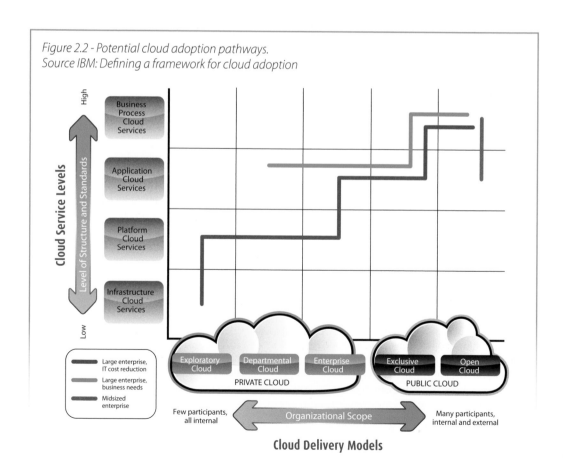

*Figure 2.2 - Potential cloud adoption pathways.*
*Source IBM: Defining a framework for cloud adoption*

So, companies need to think about a adoption strategy of cloud services. Potential pathways will vary according to the chosen delivery model and service layer, as well whether the migration to cloud is driven by the business or IT.

Figure 2.2 gives a visual map of potential cloud adoption pathways from IBM. Such visualizations can help organizations identify challenges that should be considered prior to cloud implementation.

Large organizations may be early adopters of public clouds for new services, but will more likely start with developing cloud delivery skills and experience. And yes, the question of outsourcing will be on the table again.

The goals in implementing an "exploratory cloud" - similar to a proof of concept - are to develop customer and provider competencies and create awareness of cloud architectural and management requirements. A key integration requirement for private clouds is virtualization of servers, storage and networks. (We will look under the virtualization hood of the cloud in Chapter 4.)

In a "departmental cloud", the goal is to expand use of cloud computing to users who are not familiar with cloud capabilities, and to begin developing business support systems and operational support systems capabilities.

One major roadblock will be that existing applications need to be retrofitted to run in the cloud or phased out. Large public cloud service providers won't be of much help here. They are as inexpensive as they are inflexible. Everything has to be done their way, although they do update their services partly based on user input.

> Large public cloud service providers won't be of help here. They are as cheap as inflexible.

So at this stage at least, public clouds are not the natural habitat for the majority of large-enterprise IT. However, a private cloud, internally or externally hosted, is a different story. It combines flexibility and price-tag advantages with the traditional management control over service delivery, security and compliance. The private cloud also offers a sensible migration path for existing applications and preserves investments in infrastructure, applications, and information. Most large organizations will likely follow a hybrid approach, in which the advantages of the private cloud can be combined with the access to innovative and on-demand services the public cloud offers.

In this "federated" world, a private cloud serves as the gateway and control mechanism for public cloud services, yet another reason why the private cloud is the place to start for large enterprises.

## 2.3. Preparing the Organization: Technology

Introducing cloud services doesn't require a big bang approach. Public cloud services can be introduced – at least from a technology perspective – gradually as needed. A migration to a private cloud is not about embarking upon a whole new set of activities or a massive implementation project. From a IT perspective, you can look at it as a better way to organize and manage existing technology resources. The cloud is the name for the overall coordination mechanism for a variety of technology improvement initiatives that companies need anyway, have under way, or in some cases have completed. This includes:

> Consolidating servers, storage, networks, and other IT resources

> Virtualizing technology resources, including information and applications

> Organizing and provisioning IT offerings as business services

▷ Structuring and managing IT as a shared services organization

▷ Automating technology resource and security management

▷ Building standard interfaces with compatible service providers

▷ Making effective use of selected public cloud services

*(Source: EMC, "Private Cloud Means Business")*

In an interesting whitepaper, Journey to the Private Cloud, IT company EMC has documented its own migration process . We have enclosed a short version of that in part III of this book and will not elaborate on it here, but Figure 2.3 gives an idea of the comprehensiveness of such a program.

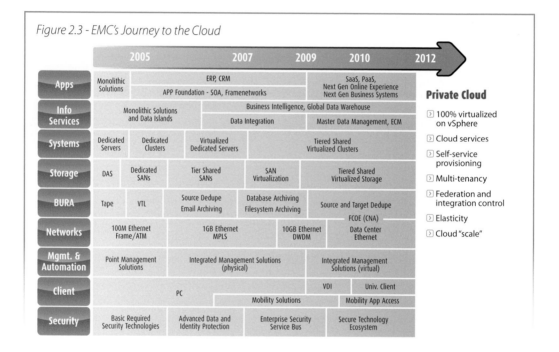

*Figure 2.3 - EMC's Journey to the Cloud*

The private cloud is the umbrella for all these improvement initiatives, and a private cloud roadmap can be the means of integrating these efforts.

## What Not to Put in the Cloud

The business value of a private cloud grows as more resources are included. That doesn't mean all resources should go in the cloud. EMC defined these exceptions:

▷ Specialized business applications, such as analytical trading systems in financial services. These tend to be complex "workhorse" systems within specific business functions, and the value of pooling these resources is limited.

- ▷ Applications and databases that must absolutely be walled off from the rest of the computing environment for legal or regulatory reasons, such as local privacy laws. Companies tend to segregate such resources physically to be safe. However, with the help of state-of-the-art virtualization management methods, you may be able to move many of these sensitive assets to a private cloud.

- ▷ Applications that have been written, and their performance optimized, with specific systems architectures in mind. This is a temporary impediment. Over time, companies may choose to retrofit such applications.

*(Source: EMC, "Private Cloud Means Business")*

## 2.4. Preparing the Organization: Change Management

First of all, whether IT departments like it or not, cloud services are invading organizations. It is happening. In almost every organization, there are "stealth clouds" that the IT-staff doesn't know of. Employees use iPhones, LinkedIn, Google Docs, iTunes and YouTube at home and expect this level of ease-of-use and functionality at work too. Self-service is how users want to interact. Users will implement business applications outside a company's firewall, if the internal IT services are not meeting their demands. Saying no is not always an option. Business users shape their expectations based on their experience as consumers. Inside the company walls, they may encounter user unfriendly tools and services with less functionality, slow or unresponsive systems, and less freedom to solve problems. A frequently heard question: why does it take seconds to find information on the Web and ages to find information on the corporate intranet? Good point.

The introduction of cloud services will have a major impact on your whole organization, not just the IT department. It will change the way users request and access applications and services. Tomorrow specific business units will not have their own servers, applications and even system administrators. Maybe virtualization has removed that mindset already. A cloud computing strategy is in this respect more of an evolution than a revolution. What never changes is that IT departments must embrace new technology - cloud computing models - while serving a diverse base of users, managing existing systems, and integrating a variety of existing applications.
Companies will all have their own and very different "journeys to the cloud". At the end of the day, the focus will be on the delivery and access to a service or application, and not on a hardware-based infrastructure.

The last decade we have had countless of books on the subject of "business IT alignment". This alignment between the business and IT is in contrast to what is often experienced in organizations. Often IT and business professionals are unable to bridge the gap between themselves because of differences in objectives, culture, and incentives.
Cloud computing is not the panacea for this, but the cloud approach will change the overall consumption and procurement model of IT to a utility-based model. This is a challenging new perspective for CIOs: the IT department is not a cost center anymore; it is a service provider that is financed by contributions from the business units.

## Change! Yes, We Can?

Today organizations can choose whether they implement business services in-house, have them hosted, outsource them, or acquire them through the cloud. In a few years from now, most organizations will have a hybrid environment. Enterprises that decide to utilize the cloud will need to make sure that it supports corporate and IT governance requirements. At a more detailed level, there are issues of emerging standards, business process management, and the overall issues of managing costs.

Companies will want to examine their most strategic business processes, intellectual property, and business information, and determine how these computing assets will be delivered in the future. Which ones are ripe to take advantage of the cloud, private or public? Which ones will be delivered the traditional way?

The journey to the cloud will be both a challenge as well as an opportunity for internal IT departments. The skill set for developing and maintaining virtualization infrastructures and cloud delivery services are quite different. A variety of traditional IT jobs will disappear, particularly since many of existing (legacy) applications will need to be retrofitted or replaced to take advance of the benefits of virtualization and the private cloud.

Therefore virtualization programs can be a natural starting point for (additional) outsourcing.

Companies need to develop frameworks for cloud adoption, specifying roles and responsibilities for both (internal or external) providers and consumers of cloud services. Roadmaps need to be established, training programs set up. The board needs to spread the message. Figure 2.4 show the roadmap the ING Bank has developed for the training program as part of the change campaign inside the organization. An interesting aspect of this is the development of a certified training program for both virtualization as cloud skill sets. This is a small part of ING's comprehensive cloud strategy.

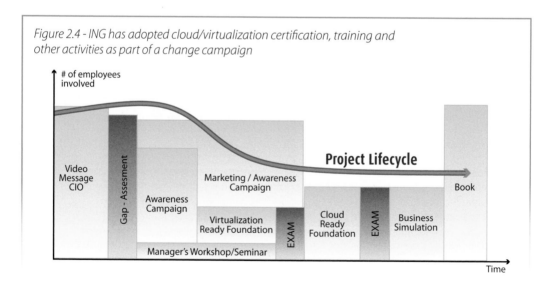

Figure 2.4 - ING has adopted cloud/virtualization certification, training and other activities as part of a change campaign

## To Begin

There are many types of cloud computing, with different service models and delivery models. According to Gartner, Software as a Service (SaaS) is in many ways the most mature of the cloud types. The Dutch electronics giant Philips for example has cloud-based SAP services. The Telekom subsidiary T-Systems provides these services for Philips via a private cloud. This outsourcing contract is part of a global program in which Philips is consolidating and modernizing its IT infrastructure.

Gartner often sees SaaS coming into an organization through departmental business purchases. Sometimes the IT department is the last to find out. Gartner: "This frequently means that IT has to clean up poor contracts, bad technology choices that prohibit good application integration, or, worse yet, SaaS services plagued with operational issues such as inadequate security."

Gartner advices companies four basic steps in order to "get in front of the SaaS curve":

> **Step 1:** Analysis. Determine the value of SaaS or a specific SaaS-application. As with any technology or delivery model, there are pros and cons to consider.

> **Step 2:** Develop a SaaS policy and governance document in a collaborative effort between the business and IT. This document should be neutral in regard to any particular application domain. Such a police will ensure consistency of SaaS deployments across your organization.

> **Step 3:** Vendor evaluation. If you did your homework in Step 2, you should have a reputable process that can be applied to each new vendor selection process.

> **Step 4:** Develop an integration road map on how SaaS applications will integrate with on-premises applications and other SaaS solutions deployed. Clear approaches should be identified (e.g., real-time, batch, etc.), including potential integration providers that can be used.

*Source: Robert P. Desisto, "Four Steps to Get in Front of the SaaS Curve", Gartner, June 2010*

## 2.5. Limitations and Challenges

Cloud architectures are maturing rapidly, but today's cloud computing solutions still have drawbacks and limitations, such as security and compliance concerns, proprietary application platforms that require redevelopment time, and the inability to move to another provider. According to IDC-research, back in 2008 security was already a major concern of CIO's (IDC Enterprise Panel, 2008), followed by performance and availability. At the 2010 RSA Conference, the buzz still focused on the security cloud service providers offer. The CSA's (Cloud Security Alliance) Top Cloud Threats Report issued a warning that some cloud services have unwittingly hosted malicious software.

So, it is obvious that businesses will feel more reassured if providers can demonstrate effective policy enforcement and prove compliance to national laws.

### Security and Compliance

As mentioned above, security and compliance rank as CIOs' top concerns with cloud computing. These concerns are primarily valid for the public cloud. Private clouds offer enhanced security based on existing best practices in organizations. All of the existing security infrastructure, including firewalls, encryption, and passwords, remains active in a private cloud.

With hosted private clouds, you have the same issues as with normal outsourcing: trust, encryption and compliance. The only new security-concern comes from the very nature of the cloud infrastructure: the fact you may be sharing cloud space with another organization. You cannot physically segregate machines. So there must be trust in the vendor's security model.

IT managers must look for the right balance between the security of an internal, dedicated infrastructure and the improved economics of a shared, external cloud environment. There is a lot going on in this arena with CloudAudits and similar initiatives.

With the public cloud, you lose transparency and therefore control. By law, a company remains ultimately responsible for its sensitive information. The simple fact that you may not know in which country your data is being stored violates some national data protection statutes (EU Data Protection Directive and U.S. Safe Harbor program). Not all cloud services indicate this information in service-level agreements, nor provide adequate audit trails.

Remember, on the other hand, that the cloud has potential advantages in terms of disaster recovery abilities, automated security management and availability. Also shifting public data to an external cloud reduces the exposure of the internal sensitive data.

## Lack of Interoperability

A serious drawback is still a lack of interoperability between clouds, just as you have in the traditional IT world, by the way. The absence of standardization across cloud-based platforms creates unnecessary complexity and results in high migration costs. Each cloud vendor has a different application model. This is underpinned with proprietary, vertically integrated product offerings that limit platform portability. There are initiatives and pressure groups that strive for more standardization, such as the Open Cloud Manifesto launched in 2008 and the Open Data Center Alliance established October 2010.

## Lack of Compatibility

Many existing cloud technologies do not offer full compatibility with existing applications. Some public clouds sacrifice application compatibility in order to provide improved scalability and other features. Converting MS Office documents into Google Docs, for example, will lead to loss of advanced layout and functional information.

This can potentially mean is that an IT department has to write entirely new applications specific to that cloud, or, at the very least, make very significant modifications to their existing applications or documents before they can be accessed from the cloud.

## The Top Threats to Cloud Security

The Cloud Security Alliance, a group of customers and cloud vendors published in March 2010 a paper discussing the 'Top Threats to Cloud Computing'. We've summarized them:

> ▣ Abuse and nefarious use of cloud computing: hackers have embedded malicious software into some cloud infrastructures. CSA recommends service providers employ stricter initial registration and validation processes.

- ▷ Insecure application programming interfaces: Businesses use APIs to manage and interact with the cloud. However, a weak set of APIs exposes organizations to many security threats.

- ▷ Malicious insiders: Large companies initiate background checks on new employees. Why shouldn't you expect the same of your suppliers?

- ▷ Shared technology vulnerabilities: Virtualization hypervisors mediate access between multiple operating systems and the service provider's resources. But hypervisors have exhibited flaws that allow guest operating systems to gain inappropriate levels of control.

- ▷ Data loss/leakage: Data can be compromised in many ways, such as by corrupted backups or storage on unreliable media. Businesses should also demand providers wipe media before releasing it into the storage pool, and specify backup and retention strategies.

- ▷ Account, service and traffic hijacking: Mitigate the risk of unauthorized access to data by prohibiting the sharing of credentials between users and services.

- ▷ Unknown risk profile: How well do you understand your cloud supplier's security strategy and procedures? Ask for full disclosure of procedures for patching schedules, employee access to logs and so on.

## 2.6. Governance

Each of the cloud delivery and service models comes with a set of governance challenges. To make things more complicated, there is no clean dividing line between different approaches. Boundaries between private and public cloud vendors begin to blur, as vendors broaden their offerings. And in addition, hybrid environments - where on-premises applications will be used in collaboration with traditional hosted services and cloud services - will be the norm. This variety of models introduce new IT governance challenges, all the more so because new powerful suppliers with attractive functionality are arriving on the playing field. It definitely makes governance more complicated. But on the other hand, outsourcing did so as well.

# Virtualization: The Real Thing

Fred van der Molen

# 3. Virtualization: The Real Thing

## 3.1.  A Brief History into Virtualization

In this chapter we take a look under the hood of the cloud. We have to. The concept of virtualization is really at the heart of the cloud; virtualization is the enabling technology for cloud computing.

Virtualization is a set of techniques that allows making a split between physical and logical systems. It decouples users, operating systems, and applications from the specific hardware they use. It makes systems far more efficient.

Starting in the 1990s, the so called "x86-based" server market, based first on Intel and later AMD processors as well, grew exponentially. In contrast with existing enterprise servers (mainly mainframes or UNIX-based servers) x86-based servers had no easy way to move workloads around. Yet because these computers were cheap and ubiquitous, they became very popular. The underlying server paradigm was based on the philosophy "one application, one operating system, one server."

*Figure  3.1 - The hypervisor makes a split between physical (server) and logical systems.*

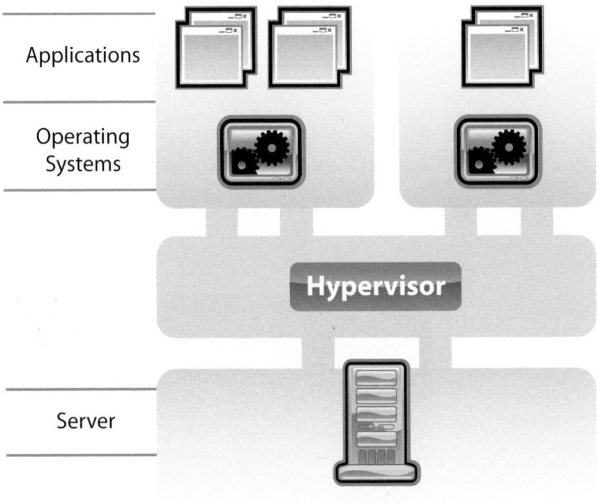

This approach came with a price: a very low system utilization. Utilization percentages less than 15 percent of their capacity were - and are - quite normal. Data centers were filled rack after rack with systems that were fiddling most of the time, but still consumed power and generated heat, day after day. Likewise, the capacity of integrated hard disks or direct-attached storage was largely wasted as well. The cost of managing all these boxes turned out to be extremely high as well; many administrators were required to maintain and upgrade all these systems.

For a long time, no one shed tears over wasted capacity on inexpensive servers; there was little you could do about it anyway. IT simply selected hardware that would meet performance demands and could cope with peak loads.

Virtualization, pioneered by VMware, introduced increased efficiency in the data center. The key virtualization layer, the hypervisor, makes a split between physical and logical systems by "fooling" the the operating system (OS). The OS still thinks it controls the hardware but is in fact contained in a "virtual machine" (VM).

This was a big challenge, but in the past decade virtualization software improved dramatically. Likewise new generations of processors, operating systems, and other server components became increasingly more VM-ready. You even can hear VM evangelists proclaim that "the hypervisor is the new operating system". And indeed, we are certainly moving in that direction. The virtualization layer is becoming more and more important, and we can foresee a future in which applications are tuned for running in a virtual machine directly.

The hypervisor, also called VM Monitors, let you run multiple operating systems simultaneously on one piece of hardware. You can have multiple instances of Windows, Unix and Linux virtual machines on one system. On large enterprise systems, you can run hundreds of virtual servers on one box. When it comes to hypervisors, there is choice now. Market leader VMware's (ESX) main competitors are Microsoft (Hyper-V) and Citrix Systems (XenServer). Due to this competition, entry level hypervisors are becoming a free ticket; vendors focus their business models on large-scale virtualization, tools, management, availability and disaster recovery software, and consultancy.

About 20 percent of new servers in Western Europe are used in a virtualized environment, according to recent IDC research (Q4, 2009).

## Virtualize Everything

Most of the time when the terms "virtualization" comes up, server virtualization is meant. But you can virtualize almost every part of the IT-infrastructure. Computer scientists started with

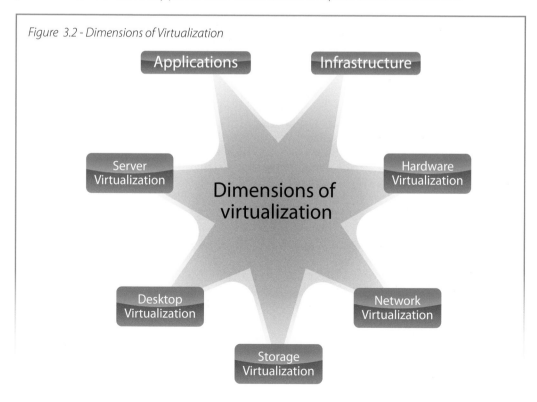

*Figure 3.2 - Dimensions of Virtualization*

Applications

Infrastructure

Server Virtualization

Hardware Virtualization

Dimensions of virtualization

Desktop Virtualization

Network Virtualization

Storage Virtualization

memory and ended up virtualizing almost everything: storage, servers, networks, applications and desktops.

In general, virtualization is a framework or methodology of dividing the resources of a computer into multiple execution environments.

Although much of the talk about virtualization involves server virtualization, other elements of the data center – e.g. storage and network - are intimately involved. If virtual servers are to move from place to place, they cannot depend on physical devices that are tied to a particular location. The underlying disks must be presented to all of the computers. This can be done with a conventional storage-area network (SAN). It can also be done by virtualizing the storage network.

Virtualization also leads to a more efficient approach for backups. In a virtualized environment, backups can take place in a central location rather than on the individual machines. This can lead to savings on licensing costs and processing capacity when engineered correctly.

The new kid on the block is desktop virtualization. In part III of this book, we have two case stories from organizations which have implemented a "Virtual Desktop Infrastructure", publisher Wolters Kluwer and the Dutch city of Zwolle.

## 3.2.   Under The Hood: Different Approaches To Virtualization

The proliferation of Intel and AMD x86-based servers, and industry promotion of virtualization and cloud computing, makes it appear that x86 is the only virtualization game in town. But in fact virtualization was introduced in the 1960s and has been supported by many computer architectures ever since.

IBM first brought virtualization to their 7044 mainframe systems, later introducing the technology across a range of platforms. Other vendors of enterprise servers (e.g HP and Sun) worked with virtualization techniques as well, well before servers based on Intel-processors (and later AMD) found their way to the data center.

### Software Virtualization

Software, or "full" virtualization, is a technique in which the hypervisor "traps" the hardware functions the operating system uses, emulating these operations and returning information consistent with what the real hardware would deliver. The bad news is that this intermediary layer reduces the system performance. The good news is that guest OS and most applications can run unchanged in such an environment.

### Paravirtualization

Paravirtualization is actually a new term for an old IBM concept. It is a technique that presents a software interface to **virtual machines** that is similar but not identical to that of the underlying hardware. Without going into details, this approach has the advantage that it avoids much of the trapping-and-emulation overhead associated with software virtualization. Therefore it can be faster. A major disadvantage is however that it requires a modified guest OS.

### Hardware-Assisted Virtualization

Until 2006, virtualization on x86-based computers was largely software-based. To cope with the overhead associated with trapping and emulating tasks, processor manufacturers made extensions to the x86 system architecture. Key hypervisor suppliers support (some of) these extensions in their software. Hardware assistance refers to two independent technologies, Intel VT-x and AMD-V, created by respectively Intel and AMD, which improve processor

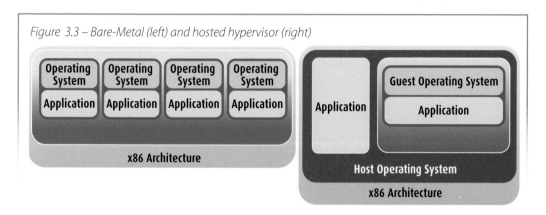

*Figure  3.3 – Bare-Metal (left) and hosted hypervisor (right)*

performance and support I/O virtualization and memory virtualization. They were introduced into CPU designs in 2005.

### Bare-Metal Versus Hosted Hypervisor

Another distinction is made between bare-metal hypervisors and hosted hypervisors. A bare-metal hypervisor runs directly on the hardware to control the hardware and to monitor guest operating systems. Examples are VMware ESX Server, Microsoft Hyper-V, Oracle VM Server for SPARC and Xen Hypervisor.
A hosted hypervisor runs within a conventional operating system environment. Examples are VMware Server, VirtualBox and Microsoft Virtual Server. Microsoft has a built-in virtualization capability in Windows Server.

## 3.3.   Benefits

Cost-cutting is a major incentive for virtualization programs. According to a recent Forrester survey the majority of the interviewees said that they recouped their investment in virtualization within one year, with some companies breaking even within a few months. While most companies built their business case on a foundation of cost savings, better business continuity/disaster recovery and faster time-to-market for new applications/services were top motivators as well.

**Key Capabilities**

- ▷ Virtualization permits a single physical server to run multiple server instances .

- ▷ Automated management tools can allocate any amount of a physical server's capacity to a VM, scaling it up and down as necessary.

- ▷ The entire operating system and application environment is stored on a virtual disk, which can be easily duplicated to create new VMs.

- ▷ VMs are highly portable, allowing IT to quickly migrate them between physical machines to allow maintenance on the physical hardware or to balance workloads.

- ▷ If a physical server fails, its VMs can be quickly restarted on another system.

Virtualization removes the physical boundaries of your IT-infrastructure. In a virtualized environment, you cannot find your resources on a single computer in a given room. Your application is a workload somewhere in a data center or even somewhere in the cloud. This might sound disturbing, but it turns out to be highly efficient and reliable. Although virtualization processes are regarded complex, the technology and management tools have matured rapidly.

The potential savings in hardware, power, and cooling investment are substantial. In fact, server virtualization is a no-brainer today for most companies. However, according to a recent study of Forrester (The Business value of Virtualization, July 2009) many companies still haven't realized all the potential savings virtualization offers. This study shows that companies have virtualized between 10 and 30 percent of their physical servers. While they achieve rapid return on investment through hardware savings, firms appear to slow down after their initial successes, with many planning to virtualize just 50 percent of their systems. According to Forrester, "upfront planning can result in increased long-term savings."

The key benefits of virtualization are:

- ▷ Reduction of costs

- ▷ Increased flexibility, speed and scalability

- ▷ Quicker time to market

- ▷ Environmental benefits

Key benefits of virtualization are:

## Reduction of Costs

Virtualization reduces investments in hardware, cooling and floor space. By making better use of IT hardware, virtualization frees up operating expenses that go toward "keeping the lights on" for reinvestment in business growth. Lower administration and provisioning costs must also be included. One administrator can manage far more servers; new servers and new capacity can be deployed easily.

Before companies started to virtualize, the average server-utilization was about 10 percent. Beyond just hardware savings from consolidation, virtualization optimizes infrastructure costs and increases operational efficiency. An stunning example of consolidation is IBM's Big Green project in 2007 during which 3600 servers worldwide were consolidated in 30 mainframes running Linux.

Virtualization leads to significant savings in cooling and floor space too. In the Big Green project, IBM was able to reduce energy consumption by 80 percent, thanks to fewer systems, data centers and cooling facilities. In Part III of this book, several case stories illustrate the potential savings of a virtualized infrastructure.

### Increased Flexibility, Scalability and Time to Market

Virtualization makes it easy to adapt IT assets to changing conditions, whether the changes are unpredictable and driven by the business cycle, or whether they are seasonal and predictable, such as peak sales seasons or quarterly and annual financial closing periods. Virtualization helps end the "one application per server" model. As demand for a particular application increases, you can add capacity to that application. You can add a virtual server – even remotely - in a few minutes. Conversely, when demand decreases, you simply reallocate your virtual resources.

Virtual environments allow for shorter development cycles, allowing faster IT delivery to business needs.

### Better It Management, Availability and Predictability

Although virtualized systems are more complex, at the end virtualization will reduce the demand on systems management significantly. In case of failure, recovery from downtime is faster and easier. Because workloads are dynamically migrated, it is easier to provide redundancy to support disaster recovery. Virtualization can also simplify the recurring task of upgrading applications or operating systems. End users will no longer receive regularly mails that servers are going down for routine maintenance.

### Environmental Benefits

The carbon footprint of global data centers is approaching that of entire countries. Virtualization reduces the use of hardware, cooling and floor space. Virtualization has a significant impact on energy consumption and carbon emissions.

## 3.4.   New Kid on the Block: Workplace Virtualization

Maintaining PCs has always been a burden to IT staff. Although this improved with new generations of computers, new versions of Windows and new extensions of the system management software, maintaining PCs has remained costly.

Early attempts to introduce inexpensive, centrally managed thin clients in the office all failed. They lacked the functionality and performance users demanded. This has now changed.  We now have the Virtual Desktop, an evolving concept established in 2006 by the Virtual Desktop Infrastructure (VDI) Alliance. The conditions seem ripe for mass adoption: the technology is

*Figure 3.4 - For every $1 spent on client hardware companies spend $3 to manage it. Source: VMware/IDC 2009*

**CAPEX**    **OPEX**

there, the ecosystem of vendors and integrators is broadening, and user adoption is on the rise.

We have in fact four flavors of desktop virtualization. These are terminal services (server-based computing), application streaming (client-based computing), virtual desktop streaming, and the virtual desktop. We will not further elaborate on this. We will also ignore the so-called "blade PC", another way to centralizing desktop computing by transferring PCs as a whole to the server room.

More important is the concept of desktop virtualization itself: it separates a personal computer desktop environment from a physical machine (the PC) by storing it on a remote central server. All software execution takes place on the server, and only the presentation layer is sent to the remote device. Access can be via a browser window, a remote session on a PC, or a thin-client device.
In this setup, it is not the server operating system that is being 'fooled', but the user. So when you log in on a device, you will see your familiar desktop appear. The computing paradigm shifts from device-centric to user-centric. Desktops are delivered as a managed service.

Hosted Virtual Desktops have ramped up since 2009. Performance problems and technology hurdles previously hindered acceptation, but the technology has matured in the last two years. Reduction of Total cost of Ownership (TCO) is a key driver, with estimates varying from 5 to 50% according to different sources. This giant discrepancy is partly explained by different starting points. If you compare a VDI-solution with a well-managed and locked-down desk-based PC environment, 50 percent savings would be too optimistic. But if your company has client/server networks in place in every branch office, very substantial savings are within reach.
Aspects such as flexibility, security and compliance are other clear advantages, with data being centrally managed and held in a data center instead of on distributed desk-based PCs and laptops.

**Benefits Virtual Desktop solutions**

- ☑ The individual enjoys much the same experience as before on the PC, but now regardless of location or device. Mobile support is easy.

- ☑ Devices (even public ones) can be securely managed. It make companies and employees more flexible.

- ☑ Devices can be simple and inexpensive thin clients. These devices have a long technical life, are cheap and easy to maintain.

- ☑ Cost reduction in workplace computing: acquisition, maintenance, and management costs of thin clients are low compared to fat clients.

## Advantages and Constraints of Virtual Workplaces

The virtual desktop model offers a number of advantages over the traditional fat client model. Overall hardware and software expenses can diminish as users share resources allocated to them on an as-needed basis. Most workplaces can be provided with cheaper thin clients instead of PCs. Moreover, thin clients have a longer **refresh cycle** than PCs.
Virtualization improves the **data integrity** of user information because all data can be maintained and backed-up in the data center. It is simpler to provision new desktops and to deploy new applications or updates.

There are some limitations and considerations to desktop virtualization.
First of all, VDI deployment and management is complex. Small organizations should therefore only consider a hosted VDI-solution. Quality of network and systems management is vital. In the event of network failure, all users will be faced with downtime. In addition, there are potential security risks if the network is not properly managed.

VDI-solutions are currently an adequate solution for task-based users and knowledge workers. The latter group will encounter some loss of user autonomy and privacy, depending on the configuration. On the other hand, it frees the worker: he or she can login to his or her virtual desktop and access business applications, regardless of location or device.
Power users will be faced with performance problems when running demanding applications such as multimedia. They require fast machines with local applications, abundant memory and multiple displays.
But when working from home or on the road, they can also benefit from the virtual desktop.

In Part III we have two interesting case stories on VDI implementations.

## 3.5.    Key Considerations When Adopting Virtualization Techniques

An organization planning to utilize virtualization is undertaking a journey that includes changes to the way people work to the type of skills the organization needs and the relationships of users with their IT providers. This is a journey that needs careful planning and a detailed roadmap.

But being a journey on itself, virtualization is just a stepping stone, an enabling technology, for cloud computing. Virtualization provides the key technology for server consolidation. The road to the cloud can be divided in four stages: consolidate, aggregate, automate, liberate.

We have elaborated on the benefits of virtualization, but there are some constraints too and things to consider:
- ⊡ More centralized IT and adoption
- ⊡ Complex management and changing roles administrators
- ⊡ Application compatibility and rationalization
- ⊡ Performance issues
- ⊡ Risks: security, compliance and availability

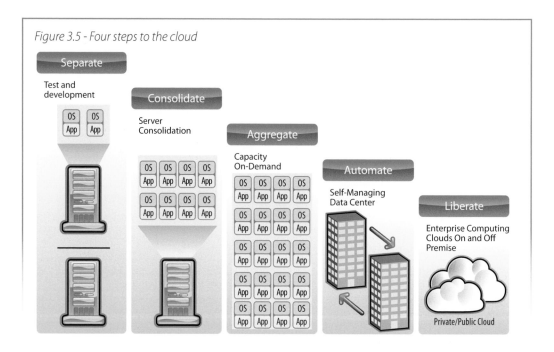

Figure 3.5 - Four steps to the cloud

**Separate**

Test and development

**Consolidate**

Server Consolidation

**Aggregate**

Capacity On-Demand

**Automate**

Self-Managing Data Center

**Liberate**

Enterprise Computing Clouds On and Off Premise

Private/Public Cloud

## More Centralized IT and Adoption

Consolidating the IT-infrastructure goes hand-in-hand with centralizing IT responsibilities. There is no other way. This may lead to resistance, not only of departmental IT staff, but of business units as well. Therefore, central IT management needs not only to prepare a convincing story, but also has to win and earn trust. A lot of business users and departmental IT staff have mixed experiences with corporate IT. A good method of winning trust is a pilot project in which one or more business units are demonstrated the benefits of the new technology and new services. Perhaps the most obvious way to incentivize adoption is to ensure that users share in the financial benefit by charging a fair price for both virtual and physical devices.

If virtual machines can be provisioned quickly and offer demonstrably superior availability, they will be adopted without any further encouragement being necessary.

Indeed, in practice this easy provisioning can be a pitfall as well. "Virtualized" organizations may be confronted with a proliferation of servers because it is so easy to add new ones.

## Complex Management and Changing Roles Administrators

The introduction of virtualization brings many changes that need to be reflected in the tools that administrators use to manage systems. Routines for software patches and making backups change. Monitoring tools that are used for correlating hardware and software events may no longer understand where dependencies lie, and so on.

The deployment and maintenance a virtualized infrastructure is a complicated management task. IT staff has to deal with a lot of dependencies: type of workloads, applications, operating systems, workloads, hardware features.

Different roles and responsibilities tend to come together. In a traditional environment you have separate administrators for servers, network and security. In a virtual environment, these roles are all part of the same management environment. This requires new procedures and policies.

Virtualization can start on a platform or departmental level. Enterprise-scale virtualization should be viewed as a new service. It will require new license agreements, service definitions, and the establishment of appropriate Service Level Agreements (SLAs) and Operational Level Agreements (OLAs). It will also require appropriate education of the workforce and is likely to need a degree of reorganization within the IT staff and the data center. This is a natural moment for outsourcing discussions to arise.

## Application Compatibility and Rationalization

Many vendors explicitly certify their applications for virtualization on specific platforms. Few applications are entirely unsuited to virtualization these days. But there are exceptions. Some are just too old, others have very unusual requirements. And some life-critical applications and real-time applications, that have interfaces to special hardware, are not suitable to virtualization as well.

A virtualization program is the moment to rationalize the application portfolio of a company. This can lead to huge savings, due to standardization and modern licensing programs based on pay-per-use. ING for example wants reduce from 2500 to 1700 applications in the next few years and is aiming at a fifty percent reduction in the long term. Publisher Wolters Kluwer has reduced its number of applications from 226 to 90 in a desktop virtualization program. Both case stories are included in Part III of this book.

Some applications require re-engineering, some applications just cannot be virtualized. IT staff had to decide in consultation with business users what to do: just keep the old situation, develop a workaround or implement a migration plan.

Keep in mind that many problems encountered when migrating an application to a virtualized environment are not specifically related to virtualization itself. For example, IP addresses might need changing in configuration files or certificates might need to be updated. Issues that are expressly problematic for virtualization include requirements for particular hardware, such as hardware dongles. Solutions are often available but will need research and testing.

To encourage migrating, it may be helpful to establish appropriate price tags for virtualized and legacy applications.

## Performance Issues

With the hypervisor you add an extra layer in your software stack, and extra complexity always comes with a price. Until 2006, virtualization on x86-based computers was largely software-based, and benefits often came at the expense of complexity and poor performance.

This has improved a lot, since Intel and AMD added features in their processor designs. However, optimization of a virtualized infrastructure still demands skilled personnel. Badly configured sessions can gobble up all capacity.

Another concern is that the virtual infrastructure – particularly the networks - will become so swamped with data traffic that performance will be impacted. To address this, it is important that organizations introduce monitoring and service reporting to demonstrate that the infrastructure is operating within capacity and effective governance mechanisms to take action when it is not.

## Risks: Availability, Security and Compliance

Virtualization introduces new concepts and technologies and, as a result, introduces new risks.

The combination of new technologies and applications can prove instable. This can be addressed by standardizing and vigorous testing procedures.

When you virtualize everything, you virtualize problems as well. In other words, with the concentration of servers you inevitably concentrate risks. The impact of a human error can be amplified, concentrating servers can lead to a single point of failure, introducing virtual appliances can introduce unknown components and configurations into the IT infrastructure. All of this calls for a strict policies, a well-trained staff, and a rethinking of fail-over and disaster recovery procedures.

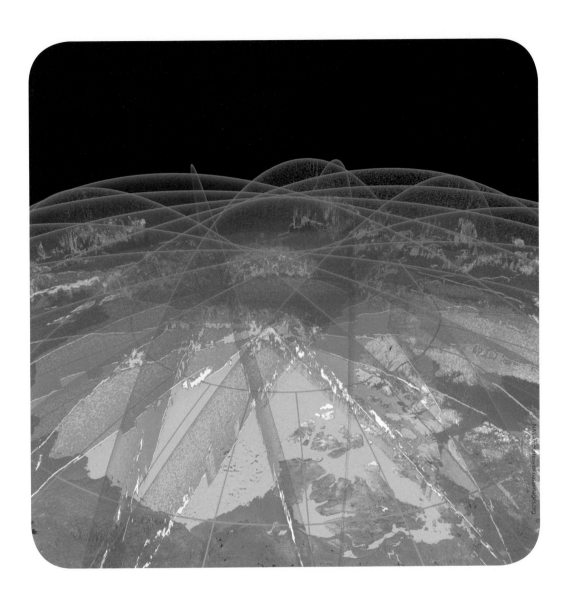

NASA/Courtesy of nasaimages.org

Get Ready for Cloud Computing

# Part II
# Industry Outlooks

# The "Consumerization" of Business Computing

Contribution: Cisco Systems

Lew Tucker
Chief Technology Officer, Cloud Computing
Cisco Systems

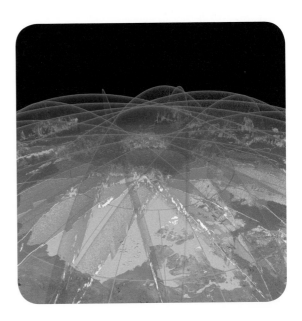

# 4. The "Consumerization" of Business Computing

## 4.1. Executive Overview

In today's business environment, success is often determined by how deeply a business understands its customers and how quickly it can respond to changes in the market to achieve competitive advantage. Unfortunately, for many businesses, rigid IT systems inhibit rather than enhance the organization's ability to adapt and change.

Cloud computing promises to change all this by allowing for a more flexible "services" model for IT systems that puts the business unit or end user at the center of the process. In this way, both the IT organization and the business itself become more agile. At the same time, cloud computing promises to reduce the delivered cost of IT through a greater degree of resource utilization, automation, and self-service. The appropriate application of cloud computing is, consequently, critical to achieve the dual benefits of increased business agility and reduced costs.

Cisco, with its extensive Internet experience in networking and data centers, is driving innovation and change to help both service providers and enterprise customers transition to this new world of cloud computing. A key to understand this new model is to look at how we, as consumers, use the application and services available on the Internet.

## 4.2. Consumerization of Business Computing

Today, as consumers, we each use the Internet to perform a wide range of tasks, whether online shopping, communicating with our friends and family, watching movies, or managing our bank accounts. However, when we use the tools and services that our employers provide, we are often faced with a less user-friendly experience: slow or unresponsive systems and less freedom to solve problems for ourselves. Why can't we enjoy the same or even better user experience from our own IT systems?

Our online experiences as consumers shape our expectations for what we should get from IT for business computing. This includes:

- Online systems that can be accessed wherever we are, whenever we need them.

- Obvious and intuitive user interfaces that don't require training to use.

- Comprehensive self-service so that almost everything – from opening up a new account to customizing our environment – can be done without having to contact customer support.

- Services are always available and perform well, regardless of how popular they are or how great the demand.

At Cisco, it's our belief that an intelligent network is perhaps the single most important part of the cloud computing infrastructure. The network determines the speed of communications, links devices, and determines access to resources. Ultimately, it is how we connect with services.

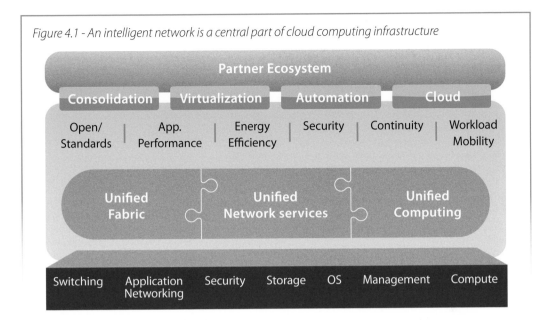

*Figure 4.1 - An intelligent network is a central part of cloud computing infrastructure*

## Everything Is a Service

Cloud computing, having evolved on the Internet, is designed to support the type of dynamic, user-friendly, self-service environment that users expect. Resources – whether a file-sharing service or a customer relation management (CRM) application – are available as services that can be accessed anywhere, anytime, through the network. Users choose the device, whether a smartphone, tablet, or other mobile device to access content and applications.

When business users want a new application, the traditional response from IT is to plan the implementation, procure the resources, implement the system, and then train users. Months pass by before the application is available for use. This long lead time can cause users to feel that IT is not being responsive to the needs of the business.

## Self-Service Is How Users Want to Interact

In the cloud model, IT systems are highly automated, so most operations can be performed by end users through easy-to-use Web portals or by other software through programmatic interfaces.

IT manages and maintains a pool of physical resources and a catalog of preconfigured applications that are dynamically provisioned on demand, when needed by various business units or functions. Instead of filing a service ticket and waiting for a response, users now get the resources they need, when they need it.

An example of self-service is virtual desktops, which provision users instead of their devices. As users, we each access a secure central system that provides a unique virtual desktop, letting us personalize our desktop experience. We can pick our favorite device to access company resources while having centralized backup and recovery. We'll spend less time configuring access technologies, such as Virtual Private Networks (VPN), and more time doing productive work. New, or upgraded, applications can simultaneously be made available by the IT organization to thousands of users across the enterprise.

Virtual desktop technology is especially helpful if your company has a large number of branch offices or kiosks at public locations. As a business manager, you can define the resources available and quickly change them as business opportunities emerge.

## One Network, Multiple Tenants

Enterprises and service providers have resources with confidential information that should be accessible to only authorized users. To meet this need, while also allowing for user self-service, the network needs to provide security, policy management, and device access control. We have then implemented a method to selectively allow employees, partners, and customers access to appropriate resources.

Policy management applies to not just human users, but also virtual and physical resources. For example, a financial services firm can set a policy that will take away the ability of end-user devices to physically store sensitive data on a hard drive or USB stick. This will help the company minimize data loss or theft.

## Reliable Self-Service Needs Dynamic Provisioning

In traditional data centers, applications are tied to specific physical systems. Given the time it takes departments to get resources provisioned for their applications, which commonly takes weeks or months, application owners hold on to resources longer than needed. This practice is often described as "server-hugging," where departments hold on to resources that are vastly underutilized for fear they won't ever get them back. Cloud computing allows system resources to be managed as reconfigurable pools instead of the difficult-to-change structures in traditional enterprise data centers. Applications can be moved, consolidating the number of actual servers to increase utilization and efficiency and reduce costs. Enhanced resource utilization brings not just cost savings, but also improved responsiveness to the needs of business units. Through the virtualization of underlying infrastructure, IT operators can quickly expand the resources associated with an application in response to increased load or activity. Fluctuations in the resource requirements of each application are averaged out across applications by pooling, allowing for the provisioning of a smaller amount of underlying computing resources.

> Our online experiences as consumers shape our expectations for what we should get from IT for business computing.

Naturally, in a shared resource environment, noninterference is also critical. Other customers shouldn't be able to interfere with your resources. A consequence of pooling is that your business unit will need to accept the notion of shared resources, with few, if any, resources owned outright.

The economic benefits of this resource-sharing model are profound: the risk of over-provisioning (that is, capital outlays in excess of demand resulting in system underutilization) and under-provisioning (that is, inadequate capital outlays resulting in unavailable systems and dissatisfied users) are both minimized. In particular:

- ☑ Capital expenses are reduced because fewer physical server, storage, and network devices need to be purchased due to the higher utilization rates.

- ☑ Operational costs are reduced because fewer data center devices, along with fewer data centers, reduce support costs, including power, cooling, and space expenses.

## 4.3.  Cloud Computing Is Changing the Model for IT

All of the above goes to prove that cloud computing changes the way we think about delivering IT services. Over time, some Software-as-a-Service (SaaS) applications might replace those run and managed by IT in-house. Increasingly, we may be moving to a hybrid model, where some portion of the services used by business units are beyond the direct control of IT. Economics is at play here. Amazon's AWS service and others now make it possible to get immediate access to virtual computing services for as little as $0.15 per hour and to storage for $0.18 per gigabyte per month. Google and Facebook offer gigabytes of free storage for e-mail or photos. These services are now setting the market price for compute and storage, which may be 3-5x less expensive than running these services in-house. In a very real sense, Moore's Law and Adam Smith are ganging up on IT's cost structure; Darwin will determine the outcome. Because of this eventuality, your IT organization must aggressively focus on bringing value-added services to you, its customer. How should the IT organization respond?

As answers to these questions emerge, Cisco believes that some things won't change: the network will remain part of the IT organization, and so will servers for unique-to-the-enterprise applications, storage of core data, security, compliance, and other essential functions. What also won't change is the ongoing stream of innovation on the Web for consumers.

This consumerization of business computing is driving a business user manifesto, inspired by the new capabilities of cloud computing:

> IT organizations must be more responsive to business objectives, time-to-market requirements, and ease of doing business for their customers.

> Systems are available 24x7x52. As we come to rely more on cloud services, network outages or slowdowns will not be tolerated.

> There is a consistent user experience across interfaces, whether laptop, mobile Web, or smartphone application.

> Price points must become competitive with services provided in public clouds.

> Because pooled and distributed resources are used, high availability should be ensured without an additional cost.

## 4.4.  Role of the CIO and IT Is at a Watershed

The business user manifesto cited above, along with the options to use the SaaS applications available on the public Internet, is causing leading CIOs to re-examine their role and that of IT. They recognize that to meet, and even stay ahead of, the demands of users, they must immediately:

> Become more of a trusted strategic technology advisor to the CEO.

> Be deeply involved with their line-of-business partners to make the best decisions regarding the use of outside services versus internally developed solutions to maximize time-to-market and reduce costs.

> Ensure, whatever the course taken, and maintain the integrity and security of data and business continuity.

> Deliver great user experiences, with increased user productivity as the metric for success.

> Provide high reliability, availability, and performance 24x7x52, without massive over-provisioning.

## 4.5. Cisco's Vision for Cloud Computing

The network itself is what makes cloud computing possible. Whether a business chooses to access cloud-based services across the Internet or build an on-premise, private cloud, the network connects systems together, which allows employees, customers, and partners to work together in a secure and reliable manner.

Cisco is addressing these new requirements through a set of pioneering products and services:

> The CIO must become more of a trusted strategic technology advisor to the CEO

> Preintegrated systems, which unify compute, networking, and storage to support cloud-based Infrastructure-as-a-Service (IaaS) deployments

> Virtualization-aware network products that make it easy to apply profile-based policy management to virtual machines even as they move throughout the infrastructure

> New network-based services, such as IP-based video, voice, social networking, and collaboration

Among customers using these capabilities is Hay Group, an international consulting organization, focused on the healthcare industry. Hay Group is one of Cisco's customers that evaluated its current business needs and its existing IT infrastructure delivery models. It concluded that a cloud computing model would allow them to become more competitive and better control their IT costs. A case study of the Hay Group's move to a hosted private cloud solution is published in part III of this book.

# Cloud Computing Payback

An Explanation of where the ROI comes from

Contribution: IBM

This is the short version of an article with the same title by:
Richard Mayo, IBM Senior Market Manager Cloud Computing
Charles Perng,  IBM T.J. Watson Research Center

*To be found on IBM's website*

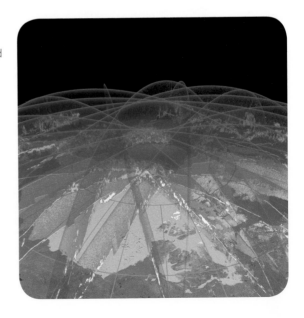

# 5.  Cloud Computing Payback

An explanation of where the ROI comes from

## 5.1.  Executive Overview

The intent of this chapter is to inform you about the five key areas of costs savings that are associated with cloud infrastructure implementations. These savings are based on the implementation of a cloud computing environment versus a traditional infrastructure. A traditional infrastructure typically has the characteristics of a single application per server with manual provisioning and a siloed management environment, which results in high costs and low productivity.

Today, organizations of all sizes are investigating cloud computing and the benefits it can bring to their company. Given the numerous claims of savings and productivity improvements, it can become difficult to understand exactly how these benefits might apply to your particular IT environment. The representations of savings in this article are based on a 2009 Cloud Computing ROI study conducted by IBM Research. The results overview the financial benefits of implementing cloud computing and provide quantitative analysis of the payback. As you will see, the financial benefits of cloud computing are very real, the payback period is characteristically very short and the action steps to obtain these savings are very well defined.

## 5.2.  The Five Key Areas of Cloud Computing Payback

The analysis of the customer payback for implementing cloud computing can be organized into five  key areas:

> Hardware

> Software

> Automated provisioning

> Productivity improvements

> System administration.

All five of these areas can see significant reductions in cost and/or gains in productivity with the implementation of cloud computing. One of the attributes and pre-requisites on the implementation path to a cloud computing environment is a highly virtualized environment. This "virtualization" will involve a consolidation of systems which will drive reductions in hardware costs. This is often the initial appeal of funding virtualization projects; however, the labor savings are even greater. Many companies still undertake the manual provisioning of IT systems, suffer long and costly delays while people wait for resources to become available, and distract highly skilled personnel from key project to focus on the mundane administration of systems. The automation of these tasks in a virtualized cloud environment can save significant labor costs while improving quality and productivity. The total savings substantially offset the small incremental increase in software costs that are usually necessary to deliver virtualization and the service management component that are elements of every cloud computing environment.

## Examples of Cloud Computing Client Payback and ROI

The example below show ROI projections from an internal IBM Research Cloud Computing study conducted in 2009. In this article the size of the environment is based on the number of servers before consolidation, for small environments the range is 5 to 15 servers, for medium environments the range is 16 to 400 servers and for large environments it is over 400 servers. Regardless of size or industry, there is a very short payback time and very high projected annual and three year return on investment. As you will soon see, the payback period is shortest and the ROI is largest for the large environments, due to the economies of scale associated with the service management software. The cloud computing savings continue to grow over time.

The first example shows a banking customer with a large number of servers that are evolving to a cloud environment. In this example, the system administration costs are significantly reduced due to efficiency gains in administration driven by the implementation of service management software. The service management software enables an administrator to manage more systems.

> Regardless of size or industry, there is a very short payback time and very high ROI

The provisioning costs are significantly reduced through the use of automation, which greatly reduces the time required to provision resources. This customer experienced a huge improvement in their productivity associated with their testing activities; however in overall percentage terms these savings are much smaller than the large savings in provisioning and system administrator costs. Productivity improvements can manifest themselves into increased revenues and happier customers over time. Those elements were not tracked as part of this study.

*Figure 5.1 - Year 1 Savings by Category*

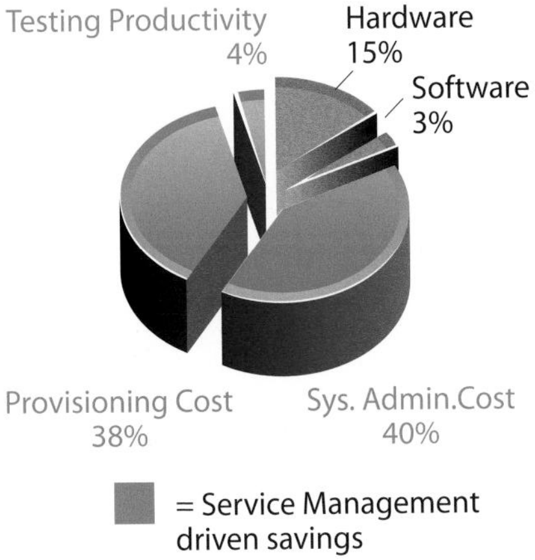

Testing Productivity 4%
Hardware 15%
Software 3%
Provisioning Cost 38%
Sys. Admin.Cost 40%

■ = Service Management driven savings

*ROI analysis example - Banking (large number of servers)*

| | |
|---|---|
| Payback period (months) | **4.85** |
| Total Initial Investment for Test Cloud | $1,313,958.33 |
| Net Present Value (NPV) | $6,172,325.64 |
| Estimated ROI over 3 years | 469.75% |
| Estimated avg. annual ROI | **156.58%** |

*ROI analysis example for a bank with large number of servers.*
*Source: IBM Research 2009*

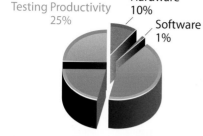

Figure 5.2- Year 1 Savings by Category

Testing Productivity
25%

Hardware
10%

Software
1%

Provisioning Cost
22%

Sys. Admin.Cost
42%

= Service Management
driven savings

ROI analysis example - Banking (medium # of servers)

| Payback period (months) | 6,82 |
|---|---|
| Total Initial Investment for Test Cloud | $302,958.33 |
| Net Present Value (NPV) | $935,880.13 |
| Estimated ROI over 3 years | 308.91% |
| Estimated avg. annual ROI | 102.97% |

ROI analysis example for a banking withe a medium number of servers.
Source: IBM Research 2009.

Another example is also in the banking vertical with a medium sized environment. In this sized environment, there is a sufficient number of servers to drive a balanced set of savings across the service management focus areas. The largest savings were driven by the system administration costs which saw a reduction in the number of administrators required and improvements to both testing productivity and provisioning costs.

## 5.3.    Hardware Payback

The hardware savings come from improving server utilization and decreasing the number of servers. The typical server in a datacenter is running a single application and is being utilized on average from 5% to 25% of its capacity. As systems are consolidated and virtualized in a cloud environment the number of servers required can drop significantly and the utilization of each server can be greatly increased resulting in significant savings in hardware costs today and the avoidance of future capital investment.

There are two main areas of hardware payback. The first is physical server depreciation. Since fewer servers are required the depreciation expense can be reduced. The second area is comprised of energy and facilities costs. If there are fewer servers using energy and requiring floor space this translates into direct bottom line savings.
The graph depicts these savings for each environment, in the outsourced case the savings are achieved through a reduction in physical servermanagement charges being billed by the outsourcer.  Typical savings in total hardware, energy and facilities can be in the range of 30% to 70%, based on your current size and annual spending. The cloud computing platform can also affect the size of the cost savings. Typically platforms like the IBM zSeries  (mainframe) can have larger savings due to their advanced virtualization and management capabilities which can support higher utilization rates.

Server consolidation increases IT efficiency while reducing overall infrastructure costs through the elimination of underutilized servers. By moving to a virtualized and consolidated

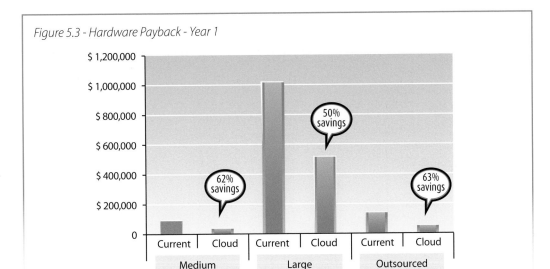

Figure 5.3 - Hardware Payback - Year 1

environment you can expect to see cost savings and also increased agility of the IT systems to meet rapidly changing requirements.
For more advanced hardware optimization initiatives, you have to look at:
- ▷ Power and cooling
- ▷ Space utilization
- ▷ Application performance requirements
- ▷ Automation and virtualization.

## 5.4.  Software Payback

Software is the key to delivering the savings. The two major components of software costs are virtualization software and more importantly the service management software that enables visibility, control and automation of your environment.
Each consolidated system will require a license for virtualization software and additional service management software. These costs are partially offset by the reduction in the number of operating system licenses due to the number of systems being decreased as a result of the consolidation.

As shown in the chart the software costs generally increase but the overall percent increase is typically a small single digit percentage when compared to the overall savings achieved in other areas.
In the case of the medium size banking customer, the client already had a virtualized environment established so they would be able to further reduce the number of virtualization licenses when they move to a cloud environment so their software costs would be reduced. The other large bank did not have virtualized environments at the start, so their software costs would increase.

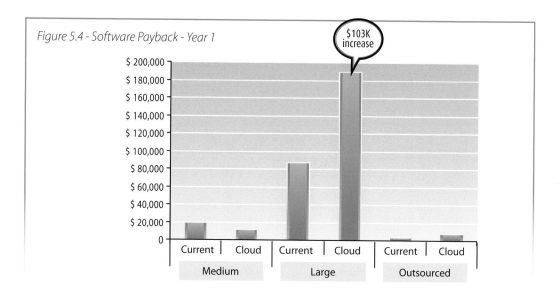

Figure 5.4 - Software Payback - Year 1

The virtualization software provides the basis for server consolidation and improving system utilization by running multiple workloads on a single server. The second step is to install a basic service management system for your cloud to enable the efficient operation and delivery of services. The third step is to install additional service management software to focus on managing the virtualization aspect of your cloud environment and gain additional cost savings.

## 5.5.  Automated Provisioning Payback

Automated provisioning provides the ability to provision systems without the long and error-prone manual process used in non-automated environments. Automated provisioning tools allow a skilled administrator to record and test provisioning scripts for deploying cloud services. These scripts can then be used by automated tools. This greatly reduces the amount of time required and allows skilled resource to be leveraged over many more systems. This provides the added benefit of supporting a policy based approach to provisioning.

Automated provisioning saves time in deploying new systems. The chart at the right shows the savings when using automated provisioning in a medium and large cloud environment which is managed by the internal IT organization and a small outsourced cloud. The use of automated provisioning tools drives the time required to provision each image from 40-70 hours to 30 minutes. As the number of images increases and the cost of training, deployment, administration and maintenance of the automation software is amortized over more images, the savings accelerate. In the large environment case the savings approach 90 percent.

Another important factor to consider is the use of standard images. As businesses begin to embrace virtualization, the variety of software images that need to be managed can quickly proliferate, resulting in higher labor costs if left unchecked.
One way to address this problem is identify workloads that can be standardized and cloned. With standardization, much of the variability associated with deployment and maintenance of unique images is eliminated. This use of cloning dramatically reduces maintenance time, as

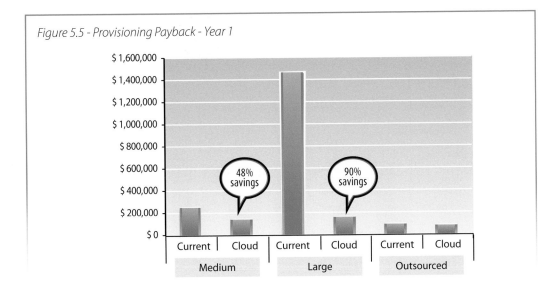

Figure 5.5 - Provisioning Payback - Year 1

the patches, testing and upgrades should be identical across cloned images. Simply stated, the higher the clone factor, the greater the reduction in labor costs.

## Getting Started

To get started with provisioning requires the implementation of automated provisioning software to replace manual provisioning processes. With automated provisioning new systems and system updates can be provisioned quickly based on policies defined by IT. Automation allows skilled resource to focus on delivering new services versus mundane provisioning tasks and the use of policies multiplies the savings by insuring that IT can quickly de-provision and reuse resources.

Products like Tivoli Provisioning Manager can help enable data centers to execute changes within the IT infrastructure more quickly, reliably and securely. Servers can be configured and provisioned from bare-metal through applications and maintained against standard hardware, software and security configurations. Computing resources can be deployed to meet current needs and then redeployed or repurposed as changes in demand occur.

## 5.6.   Productivity Payback

The process to get a new service delivered is usually a paper based process that is not very responsive to the requester. Once it arrives in the IT shop they need to figure out if the necessary hardware and skilled personnel are available. If new hardware is required, lengthy delays can ensue. With automated tools the requester chooses the environment from the services catalog which is accessed through the self-service portal. The tester specifies the start date desired, the environment, the software images and amount of time that the service is required. Policies can be defined to quickly reclaim systems when they are no longer being used. The self serve portal also enables automated workflows so that the necessary approvals

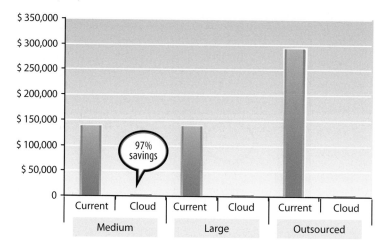

Figure 5.6 - Productivity Payback - Year 1

can be quickly obtained. Environments can be stood up and activated in a matter of minutes as opposed to days or months.

The key savings metric for productivity payback is the amount of time a requester wastes waiting for the resources they need. The chart shows the savings when using a self serve portal, service catalog and automated provisioning. The use of automation drives the idle time per project from tens of hours to 1 hour. Accelerating the completion of work has a dramatic impact on the agility of an IT organization. This shortens time-to-market and fuels more innovation for revenue generation. The financial impacts of these business benefits can be huge, but they were not studied as part of the current research.

To get started with productivity improvements one could start with two projects:
> A user friendly self-service interface that accelerates time to value

> A service catalog which enables standards that drive consistent service delivery.

Environments can be stood up and activated in a matter of minutes as opposed to days or months

Businesses that manually deploy and manage applications and IT services face a number of challenges. First, it can take weeks or months to receive the hardware and software needed to deploy many applications. Next, the cost associated with the wait for needed equipment as well as the cost to provide highly skilled IT staff members to manage the deployment process can be substantial. Lastly, significant time and financial resources are required to help ensure that the organization has audit processes integrated with process governance.

## 5.7.    System Administration Payback

As a cloud environment is implemented, hardware is consolidated and systems are virtualized to drive savings. However, one area that requires particular focus to ensure that costs don't actually increase is the area of system administration. In a cloud environment there are less physical servers, but the number of virtual servers increases. Virtual systems are more complex to administer and this can lead to higher administrative costs.

The key savings metric for system administration payback is the efficiencies that can be gained by effectively managing the virtualized aspect of the cloud environment. With the proper service management tools for a highly virtualized environment, the administration savings can range from 36% to 45%. The chart at the right shows the savings when using service management tools designed for virtualized systems.

The automated provisioning of services using a self serve portal and service catalog is a key first. To achieve even higher levels of savings and greater efficiencies three additional service management steps or "projects" should be implemented:

> ☑ Mapping the cloud computing environment so that the relationship of the physical and virtual assets is understood so that reported problems and potential problems can be quickly isolated and remediated.

> ☑ Addressing the performance monitoring and management of the virtual servers so that trends can be established and watched so actions can be taken proactively.

> ☑ Managing the cloud at the services layer and ensure that the services are meeting their service level objectives.

As the use of virtualization continues to accelerate, organizations need to adapt their existing tools in order to fully exploit both virtual and physical resources. Many of the resources that work together to comprise a business service end up residing on heterogeneous and virtual environments requiring advanced capabilities and tools to manage the complex dependencies and relationships. This needs advanced service and systems management solutions like the IBM Tivoli softwaremanagement suite.

## 5.8.    Summary of Savings and Costs

In order to determine your cloud computing payback, the first step is to gather data to establish a baseline for the pre-cloud environment. The lack of exact detailed data should not inhibit anyone from getting started. Where exact data cannot yet be measured or calculated, reasonable and logical estimates will do. This initial "benchmark" is an important component of the overall program.
 As the results are tracked, data collection improves and the savings are achieved, the benchmark will provide insights to track against. The benchmark will also make it easier to justify the investments required to get started. Savvy IT executives have been known to use their savings projections to make the ongoing project "self funding".

The following table provides a summary of the savings in each of the five areas and the associated costs.

| Area | Saving Metrics | Cost Metrics |
|------|----------------|--------------|
| **Hardware** | Reduction in number of servers | |
| | Drives reduction in server depreciation cost, energy usage and facility costs | |
| **Software** | Reduction in the number of OS licenses | Cost of virtualization software |
| | | Cost of cloud management software |
| **Automated provisioning** | Reduction in number of hours per provisioning task | Training, deployment, administration and maintenance cost for automation software |
| **Productivity** | Reduction in number of hours waiting for images per project | |
| **System administration** | Improved productivity of administration and support staff (support more systems per administrator) | |

# Security in the Cloud

Securely harnessing the benefits of cloud computing

Contribution: T-Systems

This article is an adapted version of a white paper with the same title by T-Systems.

*To be found on T-Systems' website*

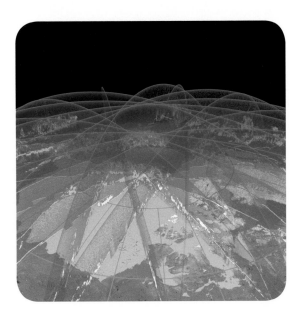

# 6. Security in the Cloud

Securely harnessing the benefits of cloud computing

## 6.1. Executive Overview

Every ICT service model involves risk; with cloud computing you do not necessarily have more or less risks but different risks. The security requirements vary between the different cloud models and from conventional models. This chapter deals with security requirements and measures for the cloud. Also legal requirements and other compliance issues are discussed.

With public cloud computing data and applications are entrusted to an outside provider. A particular risk may or may not be acceptable; it depends on the organization's security requirements. To remain protected, cloud users will have to maintain a solid repertoire of techniques for containing risk and enforcing security.

## 6.2. Introduction

The cloud is an enduring new computing paradigm driven by greater specialization and industrialization in the ICT space. Cloud adoption rates have risen rapidly on the back of the tremendous economies of scale that ICT service outsourcing unleashes for users and providers. Therefore cloud computing is a good alternative sourcing model because companies can benefit immensely from the cost reductions and flexibility it brings. Depending on the customers current infrastructure and requirements it could also boost availability and enhance quality and security.

> To remain protected, cloud users will have to maintain a solid repertoire of techniques for containing risk and enforcing security.

Cloud computing is often recognized as a flexible delivery model for ICT services that uses powerful systems and networks. It typically leverages distributed hardware and software resources and shared, redundant, multitenant platforms that deliver a high degree of scalability. The cloud is essentially the next link in the evolutionary chain after software as a service (delivery of software over the Internet) and grid computing (central pooling and sharing of high-performance resources). It takes these concepts to the next level with high bandwidth, virtualization and above all automated IT. Unlike its predecessors, though, clouds are more like comprehensive computing environments assembled from various ICT modules. For personal and business users, cloud computing offers a way to run software (e.g. business applications and e-mail security) or utilize infrastructure (e.g. storage) dynamically over the Internet on an as-needed basis. Users typically pay only for the services they consume (pay per use).

Since providers centrally pool services such as e-mail, database applications or security solutions for a large number of users, they tap into vast economies of scale and can pass these savings on to customers. They merely plug right into a sophisticated system – there is no need for capital investment on their part. Not that cloud computing is entirely effort-free: organizations still need to define the specifications for their business and lay them out in a contract with the provider.

Every ICT service model involves risk, especially when data and applications are entrusted to an outside provider. A particular risk may or may not be acceptable; it depends on the organization's security requirements. In cloud computing, where users share systems and platforms, the risk sources, types and forms will vary depending on the user's business model and how the ICT service is produced and provided. To remain protected, cloud users will have to maintain a solid repertoire of techniques for containing risk and enforcing security. Experience shows that consuming ICT services in the cloud can improve security. Many users, for instance, are unwilling to take all the necessary security precautions on a regular basis or invest the time and energy needed to maintain top quality. The cloud is a good choice for them, since established ICT providers have much more experience and highly trained personnel. The number of years a provider has been active on the market has a significant influence on data security. Major service providers, who approach IT outsourcing strategically based on their many years of experience, are preferable to smaller providers or to providers that are just now beginning to tap this field and that may drop out of the market in the near future. Major providers offer identical services to many customers at the same time and, due to economies of scale, are able to use technologies that small providers could never afford.

## 6.3. Security Requirements: Cloud Computing vs. Conventional Environments.

Before moving ICT services to the cloud, organizations should clarify their security requirements. They may wish to compare the risks in conventional IT environments with those in cloud computing. There is an instinctive tendency to equate less control over the ICT environment with higher data security risks. This is misleading, though, as a comparison of security scenarios will show.

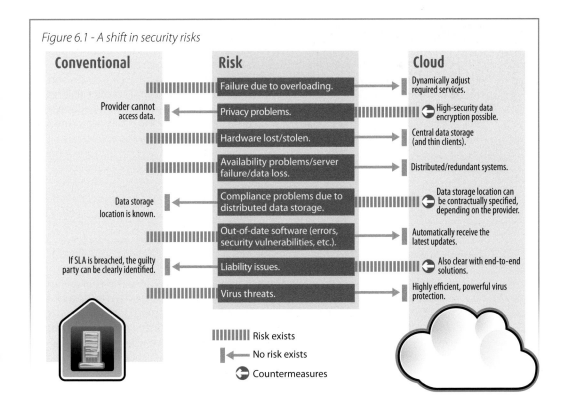

Figure 6.1 - A shift in security risks

| Conventional | Risk | Cloud |
|---|---|---|
| | Failure due to overloading. | Dynamically adjust required services. |
| Provider cannot access data. | Privacy problems. | High-security data encryption possible. |
| | Hardware lost/stolen. | Central data storage (and thin clients). |
| | Availability problems/server failure/data loss. | Distributed/redundant systems. |
| Data storage location is known. | Compliance problems due to distributed data storage. | Data storage location can be contractually specified, depending on the provider. |
| | Out-of-date software (errors, security vulnerabilities, etc.). | Automatically receive the latest updates. |
| If SLA is breached, the guilty party can be clearly identified. | Liability issues. | Also clear with end-to-end solutions. |
| | Virus threats. | Highly efficient, powerful virus protection. |

Risk exists
No risk exists
Countermeasures

Another factor is a threat's impact. Organizations are only exposed to a business risk if a threat can exploit a vulnerability and cause damage (its "business impact"). That makes it essential to manage risk and identify vulnerabilities, ideally through close cooperation between responsible users and competent providers.

## Vulnerability Management

The first step in evaluating IT or business risks is to identify threats in terms of opportunities and impacts. What specifically or generally could happen in a cloud context? Next, the organization should probe for vulnerabilities, such as inadequate data backups or weak authentication before accessing data and ICT resources. The service provider should then integrate security processes. Vulnerabilities cannot be identified without analyzing the infrastructure and how it is used, while security risks can only be evaluated if users quantify the potential financial damage and business impact.

**Security varies depending on the requirements!**

Many medium-sized and some large organizations are facing security challenges. They may have defined procedures and assigned responsibility, but security policies are still not rigorously enforced day-to-day. Requirements are becoming more challenging, too, outstripping organizations' technical and procedural capabilities. In these cases, organizations enjoy tighter security if they move IT resources to the cloud. A professional provider offers IT security as part of its core business. With its experience, more powerful infrastructure and highly trained workforce, it is much better poised to protect a high-performance data center against outside threats and run stable applications.

## Security

Cloud computing alters the security equation for data and applications. Some threats from conventional IT environments are neutralized, while others loom larger.
In a traditional server environment, unexpected demand peaks can throttle performance or even cause system failures. Cloud computing, by contrast, allocates resources flexibly and dynamically as demand changes, heading off any chance of overloading.

## Privacy Problems

Organizations enforce data privacy themselves if they run proprietary systems in in-house data centers. Providers then have no way of accessing the data. In a cloud, providers could theoretically access the data, but data encryption can effectively prevent them from doing so.

## Hardware Loss or Theft

Most people would cite unauthorized data access as a key threat. Conventional environments, however, have another, very real loss path for intellectual property: employees carrying mobile devices or USB flash drives with confidential or critical data. If they are lost or stolen and land in the wrong hands, the damage can be severe. After all, how many users have really encrypted and backed up the data on their systems? Cloud computing eliminates the risk of data loss through central data storage, automatic back up and the use of thin clients.

## Availability Problems Due to Server Failure

In a traditional IT environment, hardware breakdowns can inflict enormous damage if there is no failover capability. And few organizations have the funds in their budgets to build redundancy into every system. Cloud computing, by contrast, keeps availability high with various methods that stay affordable through economies of scale. Failures are kept under control.

## Compliance Problems Due to Distributed Data Storage

Unlike in conventional IT environments, users do not always know where in the cloud their data and applications may be. Some providers also use subcontractors. These issues can pose legal problems, particularly in processing personal data ("Legal requirements and other compliance issues"). There are, however, providers who can restrict data storage to the European Union and confirm this commitment in a contract.

## Out-Of-Date Software

Organizations that host their own IT environments will also maintain their software themselves. Maintenance is essential: every type of software has bugs and vulnerabilities that, once identified, can be fixed with patches. However, it is also complicated, potentially disruptive and can produce new errors. In cloud computing, this work is done by the provider, who applies patches centrally in order to preserve system stability and failure safety.

## Liability Issues

Disagreements over liability occur in all ICT delivery models, including the cloud. In one example, a service level agreement is breached due to technical problems. There are two possible culprits: the network or the hosted IT systems. However, it is impossible to identify which one caused the problem. This does not happen with cloud providers with network capabilities who can supply and manage an end-to-end solution.

## Virus Threats

Antivirus programs are commonly used in traditional IT environments. Some new malware can still slip under the radar, however, due to sluggish processors and infrequently updated antivirus software. In the cloud, this task can be centralized, enhancing its effectiveness and update frequency. All of the provider's customers automatically enjoy the same level of protection.

## Changing Providers

Switching to the cloud or changing providers means moving the entire application environment. Vast volumes of data and entire work environments will have to be ported. Business continuity can be assured, however, by migrating the data correctly and allowing employees to use the old and new environments simultaneously for a certain period of time. Experience is needed to maintain availability and avoid data loss during the transition.

## Potential Problems

Legal issues figure prominently in the current debate about cloud computing's pros and cons. Many organizations need to know the location of the server hosting their data and applications. If they do not, they may run afoul of regulatory requirements such as the German Federal Data Protection Act. Especially financial service providers, life, health and casualty insurers – even institutions and government agencies that use personal data for social security programs – are best served by a provider who can contractually guarantee strong security and fulfillment of disclosure obligations and legal restrictions.

## Data Segregation and Data Protection

Corporate clients in other industries also believe cloud computing holds legal, technical and organizational risks of varying severity. These companies or government agencies place a premium on keeping data and transactions strictly segregated and thus protected from unauthorized access or manipulation. They are concerned, among other things, about ceding control of their corporate data, insecure or incomplete deletion of data residing on servers, vulnerabilities in tenant segmentation and open user interfaces. Legal certainty may be added to the list if the data is stored outside the European Union's reach and jurisdiction. This is not to imply, however, that data protection and security requirements limit the use or spread of cloud computing. Organizations simply need to define their specific security needs and then assess providers' capabilities and services against them. If organizations need to know where their data is stored, they can choose providers that operate data centers within a particular territory, such as Europe. The organizations may be domestic and expanding to another country, or foreign-based and looking for a secure location to store their data.

> Professional providers can contractually guarantee strong security and fulfillment of disclosure obligations.

Permission management is one of cloud computing's main challenges. Managing users and permissions for applications installed "out there" in the cloud requires a different solution from traditional IT systems. Professional providers have the expertise and ability to implement large-scale security systems without weakening cloud computing's cost argument. To improve security, organizations can replace their static passwords with hardware tokens such as standard smart cards or USB flash drives. Whatever their form factor, these tokens come with microprocessors that support powerful encryption keys, stopping many exploits in their tracks. Users enjoy secure access to data and applications, and can even add another layer of protection with an optional PIN.

## Conclusion

Cloud computing is no less secure than traditional IT service models. However, its risk profile is different, since it faces threats of a different source, type and form. To account for these risks, organizational and technical security measures are updated continually. These updates should always reflect the user's security needs as based on his business model. Security problems only arise if providers cannot satisfy these needs.

## 6.4. Security Measures for the Cloud

### Three Cloud Models

Cloud computing has no official definition, but it does have three distinct models: public clouds, private clouds and hybrid clouds. Each one has different security implications.

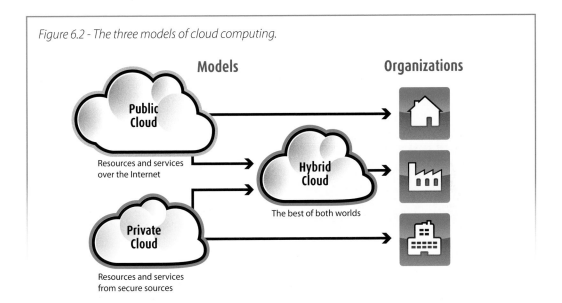

Figure 6.2 - The three models of cloud computing.

### Public cloud

ICT services in the public cloud are highly standardized, provided like a product and generally charged per use. Examples include e-mail, productivity applications or storage. They are freely and publicly available and used over the Internet. The degree of virtualization can vary. Public clouds are, however, mass-market offerings. They generally fall short of the standards of business users and are not suited for critical data whatsoever.

### Private cloud

Private clouds can involve pooling computing resources within the enterprise and allocating them dynamically to internal users. Normally, though, dedicated private clouds are provisioned and managed by an outside service provider. These clouds are designed to satisfy the specific needs of corporate customers and to provide ICT services on the fly. Specialized providers with network capabilities can supply private clouds as one-stop, end-to-end solutions. They cover the full range of ICT services and systems, from mobile and stationary devices to connectivity and bandwidth to the integration of ICT in the customer's business processes. They also guarantee service levels through binding SLAs, giving customers maximum peace of mind.

### Hybrid cloud

It appears likely that the hybrid cloud – a combination of public and private clouds – will dominate cloud computing in the enterprise space. Providers are already mixing and matching private clouds and public services to create end-to-end offerings. They integrate public clouds mainly to capture certain functions or capitalize on economies of scale. The combination can even enhance security. A public directory service, for instance, lets users easily use and send encrypted or signed e-mails between secured private domains. Essentially, public cloud services connect private clouds and utilize the integrated security technology.

## Security Impacts of Different Models

Since each cloud model is different, organizations have to decide what services they want to use, and how, based on their security and business requirements. Once an organization has decided to move ICT services to the cloud, it should start classifying its data; highly critical data ought to stay in the enterprise or a private cloud. The classifications are made as part of the organization's risk management process and reflect the information's potential business impact. Several factors figure into the classifications, including the organization's service portfolio or product range, ICT's role in it, the importance of the workflows, the organization's overall risk tolerance and the sensitivity of the data. That said, some general recommendations can be made. First, a cloud strategy should begin by entrusting the provider with applications that are not deeply integrated with internal processes. For example, batch jobs that require no further user interaction. This can include e-mail or data backup applications. Other good springboards: web applications, information services and e-collaboration systems. These are all low-risk introductions to the cloud.

> Once organizations decide to move ICT services to the cloud, they should start classifying their data. Critical data needs to stay in the enterprise or a private cloud.

## Data Availability Through Failure Safety

Availability requirements and their fulfillment differ widely from model to model. Public clouds are mainly intended for the mass market, and do not lend themselves well to business applications. Their data security and availability assurance measures are geared toward consumers, for whom data unavailability may be inconvenient, but hardly life-threatening. Not so with corporate users: they could be destroyed or financially crippled, suffer irreparable damage to their brand and reputation or lose sensitive business data. A private cloud, by contrast, is designed for business users. It ensures availability with a host of systems and activities: redundant standalone systems, synchronous replication of entire data centers, data backups and automatic system recovery after a certain downtime threshold. The provider guarantees availability, meets all data retention requirements with secure archiving systems and also offers an end-to-end service.

## Data Storage Location

"Cloud computing" is an umbrella term comprising different business models for decentralizing and outsourcing ICT services. In some models, such as the public cloud and some hybrid clouds, it is not always clear which data and applications reside on which servers at a specific moment, nor when and where certain ICT services are provided. That raises difficult questions: How do you maintain an audit trail? How do you perform forensic investigations? What data can you even process under the applicable privacy laws? And what country's laws govern service delivery and dispute resolution? The simplest solution is to hire a cloud computing provider who can reliably document that it only stores and processes the data on servers located in a particular territory, such as the European Union. This restriction provides legal certainty. Providers can inspire even more trust from organizations if they can operate their own network and do not have to outsource services.

Likewise, organizations should look for providers who institute controls and ongoing monitoring for data processing under an outsourcing arrangement, as required by laws such as the German Federal Data Protection Act of September 1, 2009. A capable cloud provider will understand the differences between legal systems. And these differences can be much more profound than one might expect. Some governments give their agencies sweeping powers to procure and process data. Yet other countries require providers to release information or hand over entire datasets. Differences also abound in attitudes toward security, intellectual property and critical data. Users should talk through these important issues with their ICT provider or knowledgeable advisors.

> Providers should be able to contractually guarantee that their servers are located in a particular territory

## 6.5.   Implementing Cloud Computing

Once an organization has decided to embrace the cloud, it should move to the next step: execution. This begins with an analysis of the provider and its services, technical expertise and trustworthiness. Preferably, it should follow a road map: first, define the organization's unique security requirements; next, select the best-fit providers; finally, migrate all or part of the ICT environment to the cloud.

*Figure 6.3 - Steps for implementing cloud computing in the enterprise*

### Define Requirements

In cloud computing, users hand off their data and applications to providers. In so doing, they also delegate their responsibility for security. But an organization can only determine whether the cloud offers adequate security if it has clearly laid out its own security requirements. They generally flow directly from its strategy, business activities and the role played by ICT and certain applications and data in business processes. After defining the requirements, the organization can evaluate service offerings against them. Security does not live in a technological vacuum, though. That is why its ICT specialists should be familiar with the latest technology and best practices so the organization can work with its future provider on an equal footing. In the cloud, security is a blend of new and familiar mechanisms and challenges. Physical and building security protects data centers. IT security locks down the systems, applications and platforms hosted at the data center. All these systems have to be securely networked within the data center and be able to securely communicate with the outside world. Data and applications belonging to different customers should be reliably segregated to prevent unauthorized access to enterprise data (multi-tenancy). Which segregation method is chosen depends on the underlying virtualization technologies and methods or other solutions.

The ICT architecture, data center locations and service models all have legal, strategic and functional implications. Headcounts and staff skills are also important, as are ICT service and security management processes at the provider's data center. Organizations should ask the provider how it would adapt security measures to their unique needs and what business continuity management and disaster recovery plans are in place. Additionally, they should evaluate the provider's policies and practices for monitoring and managing security incidents. Since the user is always outside the cloud, data should be protected not just within the cloud, but also when it is transferred between the user and the provider. This can be done with access and collaboration models and role, permission and digital identity management (organizational, technological and procedural identity and access management). Users tend to underestimate the significance and effectiveness of some security mechanisms. Take data encryption. Not only does it safeguard communications over public networks, but it can enable several tenants to share a single "virtualized" database management system (DBMS). Encryption can also render data unintelligible to unauthorized parties – including the service provider. Payroll data, for example, can be encrypted in the database so the system administrator cannot read it. Encryption can even be restricted to specific fields if not all the data is sensitive. It takes special methods, however, to securely and reliably encrypt user data while enabling all database operations to continue running without encryption. Encryption and decryption are transparent to the user and the application. And only the user has access to the cryptographic keys needed to unlock the data.

> The main question is this: do the provider and its products match the user's requirements in terms of features, service levels, other key parameters?

## Selecting the Right Provider

Clearly defined requirements give organizations a useful list of criteria for evaluating and selecting a provider. The final choice depends on the provider's capabilities, reliability, trustworthiness and ability to satisfy the security requirements.

Providers can be assessed along six dimensions of essentially equal importance:
The first dimension addresses the provider's capabilities and process maturity. They can be evaluated based on its service portfolio, its proficiency in certain technologies and the opinions of market observers and analysts. The provider's track record is another dimension. It can be checked by looking up references or talking to other customers. Information on the provider's reputation, by contrast, can be obtained from user associations, business magazines or trade journals. The assessment should also look at how well the provider's services mesh with the organization's business model (compatibility) and what efficiencies and advantages can be realized. It can help to examine and evaluate the various ICT service models. Provider reliability – i.e. whether it will meet its obligations – is illustrated by certifications and other seals of quality. Other good indicators
are company size and financial strength. Finally, the provider's accessibility and communication practices should figure into the equation. In ICT outsourcing relationships, users often stay in close touch with providers. Both sides have to communicate, and not just when there are

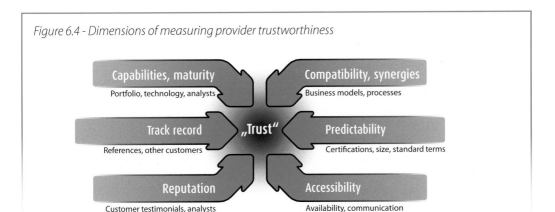

*Figure 6.4 - Dimensions of measuring provider trustworthiness*

contracts to sign or problems to resolve. After all, the services support the user's business. And as the business model and operating environment change, so too should the ICT services. The organization is essentially conducting due diligence. For its part, the provider should clearly demonstrate that it can satisfy the customer's needs better than the competition.

## Migration

Selecting a cloud provider can have a large strategic impact that goes beyond simply picking a security system. The organization has to spot optimization opportunities and hive off processes for outsourcing. It then awards the contract and begins with migration. Migrations tend to comprise five phases that should be tightly linked with risk management.

*Figure 6.5 - The five phases of migration*

### Strategy development
The strategy should reflect global or country-specific conditions. For example, organizations may not be legally allowed to merge formerly separate databases that contain personnel data. Other key factors include the type of data, the business and potential threats, including those specific to the country.

### Requirements definition
Next, the organization identifies its security and compliance requirements. Service- and provider-specific requirements are defined separately. The organization takes all relevant company parameters into account in estimating the potential impact of incidents.

## Market analysis

After preparing a requirements specification, the organization draws up a provider profile and service definition and solicits bids, generally through competitive tenders and RFPs. Many organizations consult analysts and advisers when evaluating the bids. Security issues play an important role in the selection of a cloud model. This is the phase where organizations list special technical and other security requirements and define the statutory, regulatory or industry standards to be complied with.

## Negotiations and contract

The organization should go into the negotiations with very clear priorities. That will help it decide where it can compromise, and where it cannot. The parties should also make arrangements to maintain a strong security posture during the transition. This is commonly a sensitive phase: the production environment's security measures are not fully accessible, while scarce resources and looming deadlines may cause carelessness.

> Security has to be planned from a 'big picture'

## Operation

The partners lay out the parameters of their relationship and resource provision (especially personnel) during the operational phase. They clarify details such as preferred communication channels or service and contract management. And they define quality control procedures, compliance with service level agreements (SLAs), escalation paths and penalties. In addition, their plans address practical operational issues such as employee training or incident management. Many of these issues only affect security tangentially at first. However, it may be difficult or impossible to respond promptly to incidents if the resources are inadequate or the communication channels ill-defined.

## 6.6. Legal Requirements and Other Compliance Issues

Cloud computing differs from conventional IT environments not just in terms of security, but also in terms of legal compliance. Various issues in ICT outsourcing and decentralization have been settled in the courts, including the use of service level agreements to guarantee uninterrupted service availability or term licenses to grant access and usage rights for specific periods of time. Judges have also issued rulings on limitations with respect to transferring personal data to an external provider for processing. Not knowing where data is located in the cloud introduces new legal concerns, particularly regarding compliance with national laws. Organizations may also be bound by their own policies, by contracts with customers, suppliers or partners, or by other obligations that they have explicitly or implicitly undertaken. These requirements tend to be imposed by either statutes (data privacy requirements and reporting obligations) or regulations (accounting directives, due diligence and obligations to produce supporting documents). The German Federal Data Protection Act, for example, bans transfers of personal data to countries outside Europe. Any organization covered by the Act needs to ensure that its provider only uses servers based in the European Union. And then there is a more fundamental issue: what data can be processed in the cloud under German law? That puts much the same legal burden on insurers and healthcare organizations that financial service providers face in protecting personal privacy. Tax law also puts restrictions on efforts to shift enterprise data to global networks and server environments. In some countries, taxpayers must give their internal revenue office immediate access to data on request. They also have to disclose the location of their data-processing systems to tax officials. Neither requirement can generally be satisfied properly if servers are located outside the European Union.

Contracts can address many issues, but trust matters more. The provider should cement the user's trust by disclosing who is actually supplying the ICT services. If it subcontracts work, the user should know. A provider of genuine end-to-end solutions can maintain seamless security and pursue an all-in-one approach that protects the customer from nasty surprises. The partners should discuss compliance at an early stage, covering everything from regulatory and statutory provisions to internal policies and contracts with business partners. Compliance can be achieved more easily in the cloud if the organization has prior experience with traditional outsourcing. However, the user's usual monitoring and management tools will be of limited usefulness in the cloud. An experienced provider can compensate by proactively addressing compliance issues and proposing solutions. Users also benefit from specialized certification bodies and professional security auditors. The providers can furnish certifications documenting compliance with a particular standard. The user no longer needs to perform its own audits, and the provider reaps rewards from using only a few certification organizations. Certifications have long been commonplace and essential for payment systems. They are now gaining acceptance for other ICT services, too. There is, however, no one-size-fits-all test for whether a cloud service is compliant; that depends on the organization's unique situation. After all, IT risks are business risks, and so any compliance review requires an integrated approach and a judicious assessment of the organization's requirements. The trend towards division of labor in the ICT space is unstoppable and brings many benefits. Appropriate security measures and technologies ensure that these benefits are sustained long-term.

> Providers should proactively address compliance issues and propose solutions.

## 6.7. Conclusion

Cloud computing has a certain strategic component. It is a high-efficiency model: organizations can consume dynamic ICT services when and as they need them, but do not have to invest in complex systems or infrastructure. It also has the same effect as regularly modernizing legacy ICT infrastructure since, to compete effectively, providers have to keep their ICT environments state-of-the-art. Maintaining uninterrupted operations and protecting the data and applications are top priorities in any environment. However, cloud computing's security profile differs from that of traditional ICT environments. With its elasticity, it avoids failures due to overloading or availability issues. It is less exposed to threats such as the loss or theft of (laptop) computers since data is stored centrally in the cloud. Instead, more attention must be paid to matters such as reliably segregating data and applications for different organizations or tracking where data is processed in the cloud. Each organization's security requirements depend on the theoretical business impact of a security incident. This makes it essential to evaluate and classify data and applications and pursue an integrated approach to risk management. Provider selection and migration are also important.

Three different models address use cases with different performance and security requirements: public, private and hybrid clouds. They offer resources and services over the Internet or in an ICT environment protected by the provider in accordance with special contracts and operating procedures. The hybrid cloud combines these two scenarios. Before selecting a model, users should classify their data and analyze the risks. Highly critical data should remain in the enterprise or a private cloud. Data storage and processing locations are legally very sensitive. Organizations often do not know which server is hosting which data and applications at any given time – nor the country where the server is located. As a result, they do not know which legal jurisdiction applies or if they are in compliance with national data privacy laws. Every stage – from defining the sourcing strategy to operating ICT in the cloud – should address security issues and IT governance (effective management and monitoring). By outsourcing services to specialized providers, organizations can focus on their core competencies, cut costs, and improve quality. That makes the cloud a powerful driver of long-term success. Given these considerations, organizations are well-advised to select a cloud provider who can meet high quality standards with respect to technical expertise and capability, trustworthiness, reliability and the ability to satisfy all the organization's requirements legal or otherwise.

## 6.8.   T-Systems

This vision in this chapter was delivered by T-Systems, a subsidiary of Deutsche Telekom. Using a global infrastructure of data centers and networks, T-Systems operates information and communication technology (ICT) systems for multinational corporations and public sector institutions. With offices in over 20 countries and global delivery capabilities, T-Systems serves companies in all industries – from the automotive industry to telecommunications, the financial sector, retail, services, media, energy and the manufacturing industry all the way to government agencies and the healthcare sector. Approximately 45,300 employees worldwide use their industry expertise and ICT know-how to provide top-quality service. T-Systems generated revenues of around EUR 8.8 billion in the 2009 financial year.

As a driver of innovation within the Deutsche Telekom Group, T-Systems provides ICT solutions for connecting business and society, in particular in the 'intelligent networks' growth area. As the company says: "we tap into future markets with intelligent networks."

The main focuses here are connected cars, the health sector and efficient energy management. Examples include satellite-based toll systems developed and operated by T-Systems and, in the future, convenient in-car internet access for navigation, automatic emergency calls and voice-controlled e-mail. The healthcare sector, comprising clinics and health insurance providers, also relies on the industry expertise of T-Systems. The company connects the various parties with secure transmission paths and convenient solutions. In doing so, T-Systems also supports what is known as integrated healthcare, where patients benefit from cross-sectoral care and treatment – from hospital doctors, GPs, specialized therapists and rehabilitation clinics.
Dynamically Scalable SAP Services
Besides that T-Systems is the number one worldwide for dynamically scalable SAP services. The service provider offers information and communication technology from a single production source, guaranteeing a high level of quality for complex ICT projects, especially major outsourcing contracts. Today, when it comes to supplying customers with dynamically scalable SAP services (cloud computing), T-Systems is the number one worldwide. For example, the Deutsche Telekom subsidiary has concluded a contract with electronics company Philips on global data center services and dynamic SAP services. In South Africa, T-Systems took over the ICT service provider arivia.kom, making it the biggest SAP service provider on the Cape.

# Eight Key Ingredients for Building an Internal Cloud

Private clouds: providing the ability to consume resources, regardless of where they reside

Contribution: VMware

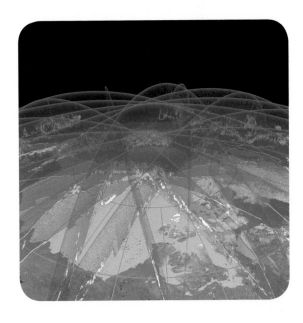

# 7. Eight Key Ingredients for Building an Internal Cloud

## 7.1. Executive Overview

IT budgets are tighter than at any time in history. But despite severe budget constraints, user demands are still escalating - as they always will. Business cycle times are shortening with increased global competition; all mission-critical applications and services must provide quick and easy scalability, while accommodating growing application access and availability expectations.

Today, investors scrutinize all new investments in IT infrastructure carefully to ensure that they match key business needs and deliver intended results in the most efficient and cost-effective way. To maximize investments, IT organizations are beginning to move away from a device-centric view of IT to an infrastructure that is application-, information-, and people-centric. Enter cloud computing.

Cloud computing technology is driving a fundamental change in today's computing industry, enabling IT managers to treat infrastructure as a common substrate on which they can provision services to users faster in a much more flexible and cost-effective way – without having to re-design or add to the underlying infrastructure. Cloud computing lets enterprises do more with the infrastructure they already have, and expand capacity quickly and economically by leveraging external cloud computing resources, when needed.

This chapter reviews the basic fundamentals of cloud computing and examines the limitations of current industry solutions. Furthermore you will learn about VMware technology and the vCloud initiative, which are enabling enterprises to move toward a flexible, federated private cloud computing model. VMware is a pioneer and major vendor in the virtualization space. Since 2004 it is a subsidiary of EMC.

## 7.2. Cloud Computing Benefits

One again: cloud computing refers to the use of networked infrastructure software and capacity to provide resources to users in an on-demand environment. With cloud computing, information is permanently stored in centralized servers and cached temporarily on clients, which include desktop computers, notebooks, handhelds, and other devices.

Cloud infrastructure can reside within the company's datacenters (as internal or private clouds) or externally on the internet (via external or public clouds). It encompasses any, per-unit-accountable, subscription-based or pay-per-use service that extends IT's existing capabilities. Clouds utilize a set of typically virtualized computers that provide users with the ability to start and stop servers or use compute cycles only when needed, often paying only upon usage.

By design, cloud computing is scalable, flexible and elastic – offering IT staff a way to easily increase capacity or add additional capabilities on demand, without investing in new and expensive infrastructure, training new personnel, or licensing more software.

## Benefits

Through cloud computing, enterprises can:

### Easily expand scalability and enhance elasticity

Using a cloud computing model, IT staff can meet changing user loads quickly without having to engineer for peak loads. Elasticity is a benefit when enterprises are growing, providing the ability to purchase infrastructure on the margin at predictable costs. Equally as important, the elastic nature of cloud computing provides a way to cost-effectively and quickly scale down a service when it is no longer needed.

### Reduce capital expenditure (CAPEX)

With external clouds, customers do not own the infrastructure. This enables enterprises to eliminate capital expenditures and consume resources as a service, paying only for what they use. Clouds also enable IT departments to save on application implementation, maintenance and security costs, while benefiting from economies of scale.

### Save energy

'Going green' is a key focus for many enterprises. Clouds enable IT organizations to reduce power, cooling and space usage to help enterprises create and sustain environmentally responsible datacenters.

### Increase end-user productivity

Cloud computing increases user productivity because users can access systems regardless of location or device (e.g., PC's, laptops, etc.).

### Improve reliability

Cloud computing can cost-effectively provide multiple redundant sites, facilitating business continuity and disaster recovery scenarios.

### Free up capacity to invest in new projects

Moving applications out to a cloud frees up existing infra-structure and resources that can be reassigned to more strategic tasks.

## 7.3.   Limitations of Existing Cloud Computing Solutions

Many of today's cloud computing solutions have serious issues, such as proprietary application platforms that require extensive redevelopment time to function off-premise, the inability to move to another provider if SLAs aren't met, and long lead times to move or set up new environments. The widespread adoption of cloud computing has been hindered by the limitations of these ineffective solutions, including:

### A lack of interoperability between compute clouds

The absence of standardization across cloud computing platforms creates unnecessary complexity and results in high switching costs. Each compute cloud vendor has a different application model, many of which are proprietary, vertically integrated stacks that limit platform choice. Customers don't want to be locked into a single provider and are often reluctant to relinquish control of their mission-critical applications to service providers.

### Lack of compatibility with existing applications

Many existing cloud technologies do not provide inherent compatibility with existing applications. Some current compute clouds in the public domain have sacrificed application compatibility in order to provide better scalability and other features. What this can potentially mean is that IT has to write entirely new applications specific to that compute cloud, or, at the very least, make very significant modifications to their existing applications before they will run in the compute cloud.

### Inadequate security

By design, most external cloud vendors typically support multi-tenancy compute environments. IT managers must look for the right balance between the security of an internal, dedicated infrastructure and the improved economics of a shared, external cloud environment.

## 7.4.  VMware vCloud Initiative

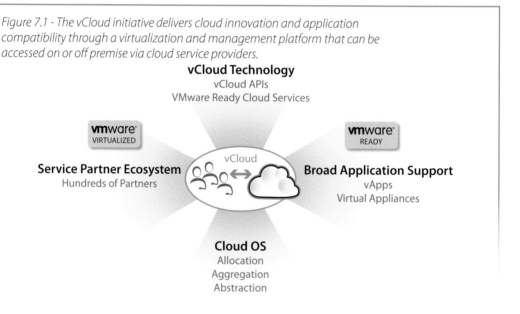

*Figure 7.1 - The vCloud initiative delivers cloud innovation and application compatibility through a virtualization and management platform that can be accessed on or off premise via cloud service providers.*

The VMware vCloud initiative delivers a cloud solution built on VMware products and the company's many partnerships. vCloud federates compute capacity on demand between virtual datacenters and cloud service providers to support existing and new application loads. It brings three characteristics to cloud computing, designed to serve the needs of all businesses that want production-level performance and reliability, on and off premise:

### Maximum choice and flexibility

VMware has partnered with hundreds of cloud service providers to enable delivery on a common VMware platform. This gives users a wide range of choices of where they can deploy applications, and allows easy transitions between providers, as well as on- and offpremise use. Enterprise-ready clouds with federation

VMware leverages a familiar and proven platform and management solution that is already used by over 130,000 customers and hundreds of service providers to deliver a reliable, extensible and manageable cloud infrastructure today, both internally and publicly.

### Broadest application support

vCloud enables easy deployment of the largest set of applications to external cloud or on-premise environments with the lowest cost and highest reliability. Additionally, with over 1,000 virtual appliances in the VMware virtual appliance marketplace and hundreds of cloud providers, deploying applications to the cloud has never been easier. More importantly, the applications that already run in the business today will work the same in the cloud, without recoding or building them on a cloud-only platform, saving time and valuable development resources.

## 7.5.    Achieving a Successful Federation of Internal and External Clouds

Obtaining the benefits of cloud computing does not need to be an "all or nothing" situation. The most effective scenario is to provide the enterprise with the ability to create a federated environment of internal and external clouds. With this model, IT managers can make intelligent and flexible decisions about which parts of their application loads they want to run internally and which parts externally - and then have the ability to change their minds quickly and easily as the business goals evolve. When considering cloud options and federation, there are three elements that should be considered. When moving applications to the location that makes the most business sense, whether for costs or SLAs, you should consider:

> ⊠ Where you want it.

> ⊠ Where it's going.

> ⊠ How it will operate.

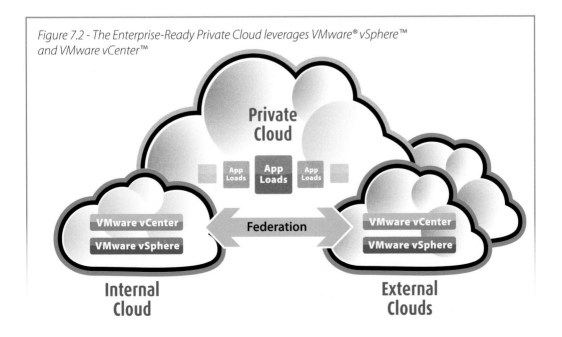

*Figure 7.2 - The Enterprise-Ready Private Cloud leverages VMware® vSphere™ and VMware vCenter™*

### The Reliable Stack- Where You Want It

The need to look at the cloud is real - new datacenters are extremely expensive and IT budgets are tighter than ever. With vCloud, enterprises now have the ability to decide if they want to carry capital expense internally or leverage external cloud infrastructure for specific company applications in an operating expense model. By leveraging VMware's reliable virtualization platform and management stack, enterprises are seeing cost savings and efficiencies through not only consolidation, but automation and optimized management. This functionality is allowing them to model their internal infrastructure as a cloud. Additionally, as they look for external providers, leveraging their trust in VMware ensures the external cloud will be interoperable with their internal cloud, making it simple to flex capacity, outsource test and development or leverage clouds for disaster recovery.

### The Trusted Location- Where It's Going

Unlike other cloud models that have one large datacenter you buy into, VMware's distributed model leverages the expertise and investments of hundreds of service providers worldwide, including some of the most trusted and biggest names in the hosting and telco business. These providers are working closely with VMware to transform parts of their trusted infrastructure, like cabling and security, to deliver flexible, reliable and proven compute capacity.

### Leading the Way- Setting the Standard

Lastly, VMware leads the innovation curve on virtualization, which has created the foundation for what is possible in cloud computing today. As cloud computing continues to define the terms and benefits it will deliver, VMware is working closely with technology leaders in many categories to define standards and set the stage for the open cloud. This solution will deliver many benefits, including enhancing solutions for enterprises looking for federated private clouds.

## 7.6. Eight Key Ingredients for Building an Internal Cloud

There are eight key ingredients to consider when building an internal or external compute cloud:

1. **Shared infrastructure.** IT staff needs to understand how to configure the underlying storage and networking so that when it is brought together it can be shared across all of the enterprise's different workloads. They also need to determine where in that shared infrastructure they should delineate between different users on that infrastructure.

2. **Self-service automated portal.** It is essential to make sure that the compute cloud can be consumed in an easy form by both developers and IT professionals. There is a need for self-service capabilities, and for highly automated provisioning portals that provide the ability to add workloads without having to go through all of the many different steps of provisioning with the network and underlying storage.

3. **Scalable.** An effective cloud solution has to be scalable. IT organizations should think about boundary conditions in a more creative way, instead using the traditional models of scalability. As a new workload request comes up, they must determine where to provision that specific workload.

4. **Rich application container.** Clouds need to have a richer application container that will show the different interdependencies between components of the application, specifically those that take place between different virtual machines. This information helps to create the correct network subnets so that the storage will work well together and not be isolated from one another.

5. **Programmatic control.** It is very common for a compute cloud to have programmatic control. Some of the more popular compute clouds on the market today have made good use of an API called REST. REST is a very simple HTTP-based protocol that provides the ability to manipulate stateful objects in a clear way.

6. **100% Virtual hardware abstraction.** Clouds need 100% hardware abstraction. This can include servers or other physical devices like storage. In a cloud environment, the user should be able to interact with the virtual machines and other devices through the user interface, versus actually changing physical infrastructure.

7. **Strong multi-tenancy.** Strong multi-tenancy involves extensive use of virtual local area networks (VLANs) to isolate network traffic between different zones in the cloud. This is obviously critical in an external cloud, but also a common requirement in internal clouds, to make sure that authorized users have access to certain applications.

8. **Chargeback.** IT organizations must be able to create effective and accurate chargeback capabilities. For internal clouds, even if funds aren't literally exchanged, the ability to create transparency in costs and services can help justify expenses.

# Private Cloud Means Business

Costs down and agility up

This article is an adapted version of a white paper with the same title by EMC Consulting.

*To be found on EMC's website*

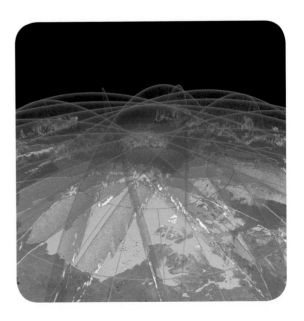

# 8. Private Cloud Means Business

Costs down and agility up

## 8.1. Executive Overview

A private cloud is a new and better way to organize and manage information technology resources and services – and a new and better way for a business to consume them and put them to work. Instead of filling predefined and limited roles, IT resources form a flexible pool that business people and processes can draw upon precisely when and as needed. What does that mean for a business? In a word: agility.

What if your business decision makers could more rapidly access and analyze a wider range of important information?

- ▷ What if you could configure the technology environment for any business initiative or innovation on demand?

- ▷ What if you could roll out new technology and business systems faster than even before?

- ▷ What if you could scale business operations up, for example to meet seasonal transaction peaks, and then back down precisely as needed?

- ▷ What if your people could more readily connect and collaborate, inside the organization and out, and easily tap into business services and expertise in the marketplace?

- ▷ And what if you could do all this while actually *improving* – not compromising – information systems security, regulatory compliance, and business continuity?

These things add up to genuine *business agility*, and that's the promise of private cloud. People often talk about agility in abstract, "holy grail" terms. Private cloud fosters agility in these concrete, pragmatic, and powerful ways. If your business enjoyed such agility, if its information technology were catalyst rather than constraint, how might you operate, manage, and compete differently?

## 8.2. Public and Private Clouds

Cloud computing is a better way to configure IT resources of all kinds, from servers and storage, to information and applications, to productivity tools and user interfaces. Through the combination of virtualization, networking, and automation technologies, all of these resources can be managed as an efficient and flexible pool shared across the enterprise. Because a cloud is managed as a whole, one can come a lot closer to optimizing its resources as a whole – getting the best mix of capabilities, performance, and cost for the business.

Very importantly, these resources are also *consumed* differently – as business services that people can access on-demand and often via self-service through a standard browser interface. Business organizations enjoy more transparency into the services they consume, and can often pay according to actual usage.

The cloud is essentially the model of the Internet, and the best known cloud services are accessed via the Internet from companies including Amazon, Google, and Salesforce.com.

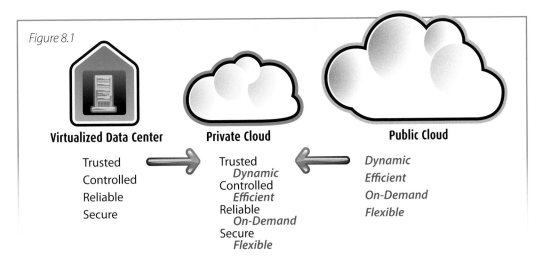

Figure 8.1

| Virtualized Data Center | Private Cloud | Public Cloud |
|---|---|---|
| Trusted | Trusted | Dynamic |
| | *Dynamic* | *Efficient* |
| Controlled | Controlled | *On-Demand* |
| | *Efficient* | *Flexible* |
| Reliable | Reliable | |
| | *On-Demand* | |
| Secure | Secure | |
| | *Flexible* | |

That's the "public" cloud, where you can rent computing and storage capacity, as well as a growing array of business applications and services.

So why a "private" cloud? Because the public cloud isn't designed or ready for enterprise IT. We see corporations making increasing but selective use of public cloud services. But, as IT executives well know, the public cloud isn't the place for sensitive data or business-critical applications. It lacks the security, reliability, and management controls essential for both regulatory compliance and business performance. And existing applications must be retrofitted to run in the public cloud.

A private cloud gains the flexibility and cost advantages of the cloud model, but under the management control of the enterprise. It combines the benefits of in-house computing – trusted, controlled, reliable, secure – with those of the cloud – dynamic, efficient, on-demand, flexible. Private cloud offers a migration path for existing applications and preserves investments in infrastructure, applications, and information, while putting all of these resources to much more efficient, effective, and agile business use.

> So why a "private" cloud? Because the public cloud isn't designed or ready for enterprise IT

To combine the best of both worlds, a private cloud can serve as a gateway to the public cloud, enabling a business to make use of the growing array of services available there, while keeping business-critical information systems "inside."

## 8.3.  Benefits of Private Cloud

The cost benefits of private cloud are dramatic, to say the least. Consolidation, virtualization, and automation can together cut data center costs in half, including a 30% reduction in power consumption and cooling costs. This smaller carbon footprint is the foundation for "green" IT. By pooling and centrally managing assets, a private cloud delivers economies of scale, better resource utilization, reductions in capital outlay, and ongoing operational efficiencies. Then there's the recurring savings from much faster and more efficient provisioning of technology services.

Private cloud puts technology resources "where the business action is." For example, with a private cloud working for it, a business can:

> **Make faster and better decisions.** Employees can quickly gather information for analysis and decision making, and they can access information and applications securely from wherever they happen to be working. Individual productivity rises.

> **Innovate faster.** You can assemble the technology and information infrastructure for any business initiative or experiment on-demand. That means faster time to market, or "fast fail" of innovations that aren't going to pan out.

> **Scale up innovations – or everyday operations – in record time.** If you're launching a new product, finding that a marketing promotion is unexpectedly successful, reaching a seasonal peak of business activity, or just closing the monthly books, your computing capacity and information systems can automatically scale to cover increasing (then receding) demand.

Meantime, private cloud also improves the performance and work mix of the IT organization. Less time and effort go into commodity activities in the data center and helpdesk, and more time and effort are available for business innovation and improvement projects. IT may be able to break out of the common rut of expending 70% of its energy "keeping the lights on" instead of working on new business initiatives.

Here's another way to look at the benefits. The private cloud approach reduces – and sometimes even eliminates – some basic and longstanding business tradeoffs. You can now have both scale *and* flexibility. You can have both low cost *and* speed to results. You can have both connectability *and* security.

## 8.4.  Cost, Business Performance, and IT Performance

We've already listed many of the basic advantages of cloud computing. Now let's explore what they mean for a business. We group the benefits into three categories: cost, business performance, and IT performance.

| Benefits of the cloud approach | | |
|---|---|---|
| Cost and Cost Structure | Business Performance and Agility | IT Performance and Agility |
| > Servers | > Accessibility | > Service Delivery |
| > Storage | > Scaling | > Cost |
| > Network | > Innovation | > Speed |
| > Facilities | > Solutions Deployment | > Efficiency |
| > Energy | > Collaboration | > Innovation |
| > Staff | > Security and Business Continuity | > Business Relationships |
| > Operations | | > Work Mix |
| > Software Licensing and Maintenance | | |
| > Technology Deployment | | |
| > Capital Outlay | | |

## Cost and Cost Structure

This includes not only direct cost reduction, but also cost avoidance and improving cost structure. Much of the short-term cost reduction comes through consolidation of hardware and virtualization of digital assets. Companies can see overall reductions of 40% in data center costs, including a 30% reduction in power consumption and cooling costs. This smaller carbon footprint is the foundation for "green" IT. Data centers have traditionally been overbuilt to handle peak capacity requirements, with as little as 10-15% of capacity regularly used. Virtualization enables you to size the data center closer to average capacity, not the worst case. And when things get busy, resources are automatically channeled to the most important business activities.

Since large companies are still in the process of consolidating, virtualizing, and automating technology resource management, they have yet to appreciate the ongoing cost reduction that a fully implemented private cloud delivers. These operational efficiencies – including flexible, dynamic, "zero touch" resource management processes – can yield a 30% cost reduction.

## Representative Cost Benefits

By pooling and centrally managing assets, a private cloud delivers economies of scale, better resource utilization, reductions in capital outlay, ongoing operational efficiencies, and the conversion of fixed costs to variable (whenever you tap into the public cloud and pay only for services consumed).

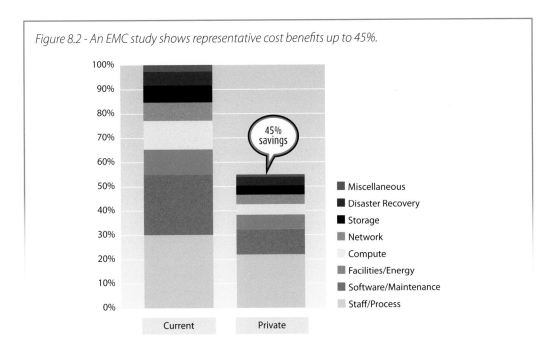

*Figure 8.2 - An EMC study shows representative cost benefits up to 45%.*

Private cloud can enable all of a company's technology-dependent business processes to operate more efficiently, with faster cycle time, and at lower cost. Benefits include:

- **Expanded access to information and applications.**
  Employees can quickly gather information for analysis and decision making, and they can access information and applications securely from wherever they happen to be working. Individual productivity rises.

- **Rapid scaling of business operations up and down.**
  If you're closing the monthly books, reaching a seasonal peak of business activity, or finding that a marketing promotion is unexpectedly successful, your computing capacity and information systems can automatically scale to cover increasing (then receding) demand.

- **Rapid business innovation.**
  You can assemble the technology and information infrastructure for any business initiative or experiment on-demand. That means faster time to market, or "fast fail" of innovations that aren't going to pan out. One company calls this "private cloud in a box" – servers, storage, browser interface, and management software instantly available for any development and test effort.

- **Rapid deployment of new business capabilities.**
  When an innovation proves successful, or for any business change initiative, the information and technology components can be quickly assembled, scaled up, and integrated with related business applications. We see reductions of over 70% in the technology deployment time, effort, and cost associated with business initiatives.

- **Expanded coordination and collaboration.**
  Within the business, its people, organizations, processes, and information systems are better able to connect and work together. For multinational corporations, private cloud can facilitate the globalization of operations and infrastructure. Outside the business, a private cloud is a platform for more seamless collaboration with customers and business partners, as well as for access to public cloud services and other business capabilities in the marketplace.

- **Better compliance, security, and continuity.**
  The virtualized and automatically managed environment of a private cloud enables better compliance with information management and privacy regulations (because duplication is reduced and the rules for information access and use are packaged into the virtual containers), more secure remote access to corporate information and systems (because sensitive assets don't reside on mobile devices), and faster and more reliable backup and recovery of information systems (because backup locations are flexible and resources are diverted as needed to recovery operations).

## 8.5. How to Proceed

We call private cloud "new" because the capabilities, both technical and managerial, to execute this approach have only recently come together. However, major components of private cloud have been around for years, and chances are you're already implementing many of them. If you're consolidating, virtualizing, and automating the management of technology resources; if you're provisioning IT offerings as business services or organizing IT as a shared services organization; if you're building more security into information and applications themselves in addition to your perimeter firewalls – then you're already on your way. Private cloud is a natural extension of all these improvement initiatives.

In the remainder of your journey to private cloud, you'll need to cover the necessary bases: setting business objectives and taking cost and performance benchmarks, establishing program management to guide the initiatives and stakeholder management to keep the right people incorporated, implementing technological changes in virtualization and automation, organizing IT offerings as business services and rationalizing applications and data along the way, and establishing governance and management controls. A private cloud *roadmap* – showing how the pieces come together in pursuit of specific business goals – can integrate these efforts and accelerate and amplify their benefits.

> Major components of private cloud have been around for years, and chances are you're already implementing many of them.

What's your next step? It depends on where your computing environment is today:

- ▷ **Still siloed.** Virtualization has barely begin, and many IT resources are attached to local business units and struggling to work together. You need to find a champion who appreciates the business benefits of private cloud, and to prove the concept by deploying simple cloud-based services to fill unmet business needs.

- ▷ **Partly virtualized but stalled.** The "low-hanging fruit" of server and storage virtualization has been picked, but progress has slowed because other resources aren't ready. Now you need to get programmatic, by detailing your road map, and committed, by making virtualization and inclusion in the private cloud the default (not exception) for technology resources.

- ▷ **Virtualized but not optimized.** Half or more of IT resources are virtualized, and significant cost benefits have been realized, but other business benefits – access, flexibility, innovation, security, collaboration – have not. You need to focus on pursuit of the business objectives of private cloud; to learn to integrate, automate, and manage the computing environment as a whole; and probably to step back and rationalize more of your IT portfolio.

A successful journey to private cloud is really about anticipation, and your roadmap documents what you anticipate: steps to take; their sequence and interdependencies and iterations; stakeholders and how to incorporate them; likely obstacles and how to remove them; and the pragmatics of staffing, funding, timetables and milestones. The remainder of your journey to private cloud will likely be challenging – but well worth the effort. With a good roadmap, you can proceed with confidence.

## 8.6. The Right Time

We believe the time is right for enterprise computing to move to private cloud, for three reasons:

- ▷ Businesses are in need of cost, performance, innovation, and agility boosts. Private cloud is simply the right approach for businesses today.

- ▷ The technologies and techniques are available and proven. EMC, Cisco, and VMware have teamed to make your technological implementation straightforward. EMC

Consulting stands ready to help you develop your roadmap and make your operational and organizational implementation straightforward as well.

▷ Many enterprises are at a decision point. As we emerge from this recession, you probably have some catching up and reinvesting to do, including in IT. Do you patch a few cracks and put a fresh coat of paint on a conventional, fragmented and inefficient computing environment? Or do you seize the opportunity to configure your private cloud and unleash new forms of business agility?

# Everything as a Service, IT too

Organizational, compliance and security issues of cloud computing

Contribution: HP

This chapter is based on the article
"Making the Cloud Relevant",
by Keith Jahn, director in the office of the CTO
for HP Software & Solutions

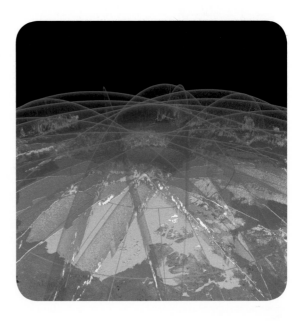

# 9. Everything as a Service, IT too

Organizational, compliance and security issues of cloud computing

## 9.1. Executive Overview

This article explores a scenario that IT organizations could face in the not too distant future, brought about by the advent of the cloud phenomena - one that forces radical change or results in awful consequences for IT as we know it, and perhaps even removing the function altogether. And if IT organizations are removed, this will - quite obviously - have a significant impact on the entire technology supply chain.

The history of cloud computing started in the nineties with the web. We're now entering phase 3 of internet-based computing. Ultimately the cloud will usher in new business models that will, in turn, force IT to reinvent itself in order to remain relevant to the business in the emerging service-oriented economy. This means that IT must move away from its exclusive focus on delivery and management of assets and toward creating a world-class supply chain of business services.

This article focuses on the organizational, compliance and security issues that are at stake, when moving to the cloud.

## 9.2. Cloud 1

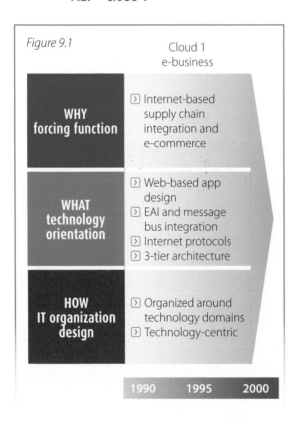

Figure 9.1

Cloud 1
e-business

**WHY**
**forcing function**
- Internet-based supply chain integration and e-commerce

**WHAT**
**technology**
**orientation**
- Web-based app design
- EAI and message bus integration
- Internet protocols
- 3-tier architecture

**HOW**
**IT organization**
**design**
- Organized around technology domains
- Technology-centric

1990   1995   2000

The cloud is not new. It's been around for years now, starting with what many now refer to as the "Internet era." This was the first generation/version of cloud. Let us call it cloud 1. It was an enabler that originated in the enterprise. Commercial use of the Internet revolutionized supply chain management processes and brought about new shopping experiences for consumers. Over time, these technologies became mainstream and fundamentally changed the IT architectural landscape.

We moved from two-tier to three-tier architectures, embraced externally hosted applications and transitioned to internet protocols and development techniques internally as a means of delivering solutions. And this ecosystem made its way through the entire portfolio of IT capabilities, solving new problems and driving efficiency gains into old ones. As an offshoot of this, the enterprise-oriented technologies moved out of the computer room and into the living room of the employees as they became internet shoppers and searchers. How long did this take? Maybe five years - give or take a year.

## 9.3.    Cloud 2

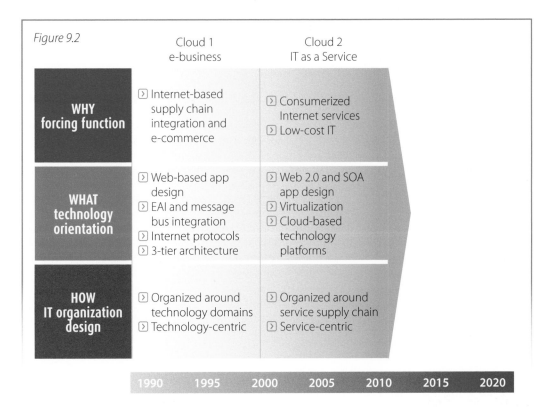

Figure 9.2

| | Cloud 1<br>e-business | Cloud 2<br>IT as a Service |
|---|---|---|
| **WHY**<br>forcing function | ▸ Internet-based supply chain integration and e-commerce | ▸ Consumerized Internet services<br>▸ Low-cost IT |
| **WHAT**<br>technology orientation | ▸ Web-based app design<br>▸ EAI and message bus integration<br>▸ Internet protocols<br>▸ 3-tier architecture | ▸ Web 2.0 and SOA app design<br>▸ Virtualization<br>▸ Cloud-based technology platforms |
| **HOW**<br>IT organization design | ▸ Organized around technology domains<br>▸ Technology-centric | ▸ Organized around service supply chain<br>▸ Service-centric |

1990    1995    2000    2005    2010    2015    2020

The current generation of cloud services is driven by consumer experiences. Internet-based shopping, search, and countless other services have brought about a new economic model and introduced new technologies. Services can be self-sourced, remotely and virtually from any device and delivered immediately. Infrastructure and applications can be sourced as services in an on-demand manner. This consumer-oriented model is forcing its way back into the enterprise on the backs of employees.

Most of the attention around cloud services in the enterprise today is focused on the new techniques and sourcing alternatives for IT capabilities - IT as a service. Using standardized, highly virtualized infrastructure and applications, IT can drive higher degrees of automation and consolidation, thus reducing the cost of maintaining existing solutions and delivering new ones. In addition, externally supplied infrastructure, software, and platform services are delivering capacity augmentation and a means of using operating expense funding instead of capital.

This cloud service orientation is also spawning new ideas for business innovation in the enterprise. Meanwhile, business people are attempting to further exploit this service orientation to remove complexity and barriers in their monolithic processes. They read about examples; they visualize new opportunities and approaches but are typically "held hostage" by their IT department and the inherent latency of project-driven processes required to make it happen. And missing the IT planning window can add years to the cycle time of getting the desired results. This is adding stress to the already tenuous relationship between IT and the business IT services.

While many companies are wrestling with the technology transitions required to move from cloud 1 and 2, the volume of services in the commercial cloud marketplace is increasing, propagation of data into the cloud is occurring, and Web 3.0/semantic Web IT is maturing. And because of this, we are just starting to see the next generation of cloud materialize: cloud 3.

## 9.4. Cloud 3

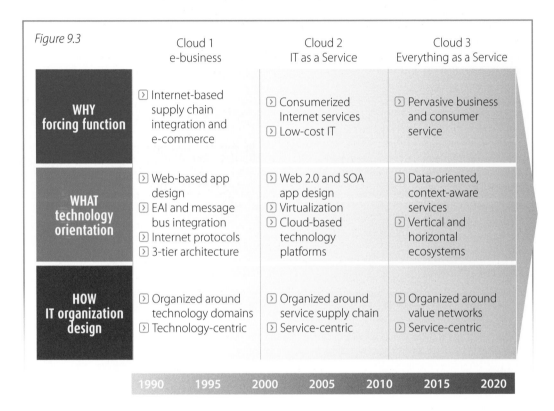

Figure 9.3

| | Cloud 1<br>e-business | Cloud 2<br>IT as a Service | Cloud 3<br>Everything as a Service |
|---|---|---|---|
| **WHY**<br>forcing function | ▸ Internet-based supply chain integration and e-commerce | ▸ Consumerized Internet services<br>▸ Low-cost IT | ▸ Pervasive business and consumer service |
| **WHAT**<br>technology orientation | ▸ Web-based app design<br>▸ EAI and message bus integration<br>▸ Internet protocols<br>▸ 3-tier architecture | ▸ Web 2.0 and SOA app design<br>▸ Virtualization<br>▸ Cloud-based technology platforms | ▸ Data-oriented, context-aware services<br>▸ Vertical and horizontal ecosystems |
| **HOW**<br>IT organization design | ▸ Organized around technology domains<br>▸ Technology-centric | ▸ Organized around service supply chain<br>▸ Service-centric | ▸ Organized around value networks<br>▸ Service-centric |

| 1990 | 1995 | 2000 | 2005 | 2010 | 2015 | 2020 |
|---|---|---|---|---|---|---|

The next version of cloud will enable access to information through services that are set in the context of the consumer experience. This is significantly different: it means that data will be separated from applications. Processes can be broken into smaller pieces and automated through a collection of services, woven together with access to massive amounts of cloud-based data. It removes the need for large-scale, complex applications that are built around monolithic processes. Changes can be accomplished by refactoring service models and integration achieved by subscribing to new data feeds. This will create new connections, new capabilities, and new innovations surpassing those of today.

## 9.5.    Which Cloud Should IT Focus on Today?

IT organizations are still struggling to understand how to utilize technologies associated with cloud 2. Discussions and debates about the how/what/why of virtualization, private cloud, infrastructure-as-a-service, software-as-a-service, and platform-as-a-service are occurring each and every day.

The reality is that by focusing attention here, we will miss the forest for the trees. Taking a technology-oriented approach to cloud will only exacerbate existing problems over time. One reason is because technology can only be calibrated to cost - thus the anchor IT metric: total cost of ownership (TCO).

Cloud 3 is not so much about delivering cost reduction through technology as it is about value. It is about services that people are willing to pay for because of the direct and visible benefit they provide.

Cloud 3 services offer businesses opportunities to solve existing problems in new ways or to solve problems that could not be solved till now. As more cloud 3 services materialize, businesses will not wait in line for IT projects to deliver them. Instead, equipped with two very powerful tools - an internet connection and a credit card - they will be able to circumvent IT to get the desired results, diverting precious innovation funding away from IT budgets.

> Cloud 3 is not so much about delivering cost reduction through technology as it is about value.

Therefore, it is vital that IT leaders start focusing on reinventing themselves. Transforming to a model where 90 percent of the deliverables still flow through a project-oriented pipeline will not lend itself to competing in the new economy. In the not too distant future, the business will not want IT projects that deliver applications; it will not want to invest in IT assets. So, what will it want?

### It's All About the Service

People in the business just want services. They want the right technology-enabled services that help them get their job done, and that help broaden their horizons into new opportunities.

But here is the problem: the traditional role of IT has been to deliver and manage technology-based capabilities that are an aggregation of assets such as applications, databases, networks, storage, and servers. IT is typically organized around the various technology domains, taking in new work via project requests and moving it through a plan-build-run lifecycle. This delivery-oriented, technology-centric approach to IT has inherent latency built into the model, which has, in turn, created an ever-increasing tension between itself and the business IT serves.

Cloud 3 is not driven by technology delivery. It is led by sourcing and consuming services. And the operating model around these services is flexible, elastic, and on-demand. The sourcing is simple, self-sourced, pay as you go. The project request gate standing between a consumer and the value delivery has been replaced by a simple credit card transaction. This does not fit inside the traditional IT model envelope. In fact, it challenges all aspects of IT - and makes people really nervous. But commercial cloud service providers get it. They are building and expanding around this new operating model and are rapidly becoming the chief competitors with the internal IT department.

So, how will IT compete in the service economy?

One school of thought is that by waving the security, compliance, and availability banners, IT will not have to compete with external providers. And this might be true - for a little while. But the cloud will ultimately force wholesale change for IT, shifting the focus from technology delivery to service sourcing and consumption - transforming IT into a service-centric organization.

> One school of thought is that by waving the security, compliance, and availability banners, IT will not have to compete with external providers.
> This might be true - for a while.

Some people could say that the cloud is hype, a fallacy, a replay of utility computing or web hosting on steroids. There are too many security issues, too many reliability concerns with technology-enabled services over the internet. That is not the point. The point is that the consumption model for business services is changing; yet as an industry, IT remains focused on the delivery and management of technology assets.

Even more relevant is that there is a next wave on the horizon that is focused on propagation of massive amounts of data delivered via context-aware services. Unfortunately, the operating model and structure of the IT organization is not designed to address the needs associated with this next wave.

IT must reinvent itself, organizing in such a way that it becomes the central service-sourcing control point for the enterprise, or else realize that the business will source them on their own. Doing so will help ensure that IT can maintain the required service levels and integrations. In order to get there, changes to behavior, cultural norms, and organizational models are required, and for many this will be viewed as too painful and too expensive.

And if the lines of business continue to go around their IT departments to self-source services, the core customer of IT suppliers will lose its buying power. The IT department will be forced into a situation where they are maintaining self-sourced services from the business. There are legitimate barriers that stand in the way of mainstream cloud 3 acceptance (security, reliability, and so on) in the business - but time and maturity have a way of resolving issues and breaking down barriers.

## 9.6.    Cloud Forces a Service-Centric IT Organization

In order to survive, IT must transform itself from an asset-focused or technology-centric delivery organization (providing and managing assets) into the strategic service-sourcing control point for the enterprise. I call this the service-centric model. This means that IT has to fundamentally change what it does for the business and how IT gets it done. And this is hard work.

Service-centric represents an advanced state of maturity for the IT function, enabling it to operate as a business function - a service provider, deliberately structured around a set of products that customers value and are therefore willing to pay for. The deliverables of the service-centric IT organization are technology-enabled, pre-integrated services. Technology-enabled services are comprised of the full roster of technologies and capabilities that, when aggregated together, can be calibrated to business value. For example, an order management service is comprised of application services, infrastructure services (storage, compute, and network), data services, security services, and one specific SLA target. These services come into being as part of the business strategy and are organized into a service portfolio.

The service-centric model will remove some existing roles and generate new ones within the IT organization. For example, service managers will be vital to packaging, pricing, and sourcing the deliverables, and business relationship managers will be needed to oversee supply and demand planning for services. In addition, existing roles will change in scope and areas of responsibility. For example, governance functions like a PMO might be tasked with overseeing the sourcing strategy for the IT function - that is, which are in-sourced and which are out-sourced.

What emerges is a more nimble, agile IT organization, one that can quickly respond to changing business needs based on actual consumption, and can compete head-on with commercial providers in the cloud service marketplace.

> What emerges is a more nimble, agile IT organization, one that can quickly respond to changing business needs

It would be unwise for IT organizations to focus exclusively on positioning themselves to adopt and implement cloud technology. By doing so, IT will feed the growth in "shadow sourcing" of services within the business functions. Unlike shadow IT, where assets purchased by the business can be discovered on the network, cloud services are not easily detectable using traditional IT methods. Instead, a more effective approach is to focus on transforming the IT organization into a service-centric model, one that is able to source, integrate, and manage services with world-class efficiency. Doing so will prepare IT to support new business models while, at the same time, utilizing new technological breakthroughs in a manner that adds value to both the top and bottom line of their business.

## 9.7.   Organizational, Compliance and Security Issues

When moving to the cloud, organizational, compliance and security issues are at stake. Let's take a quick look at the organization change first. Your organization is of course a little different from almost all the others out there: you work in siloed structures, and specifically your IT organizations are very structured around areas of expertise.

Cloud will forge a dramatic change in the way users access and request applications and services, and that will force a change in the responsiveness expected and offered, and very specifically in the way your business will operate – gone will be the day where specific business units "owned" their servers and applications, and to some extent virtualization in the server and storage areas will have removed that mindset, but the new thinking will focus completely on the delivery and access to a service or application, and not a server and associated infrastructure.

The second and very important change is: the overall consumption and procurement model of the IT organizations is set to change – project-based procurement will be lost in favor of a utility-based model with very rapid provisioning – indeed the opportunity is now very real to have capacity ready to implement in minutes, but only pay for the use of it when actually used. That also predicates a change in the relationship with your suppliers – real partnerships will become the order of the day, and procurement decisions will be based not only on immediate acquisition pricing, but actual overall financial benefits – the vendor/customer relationship will need to transcend that to become a full partnership because the cost benefits of cloud will only fully be realized with a move to greater standards based models.

Let's look at the topic that is really top of mind presently though when looking at any cloud initiative: security and by implication compliance.

## Top Threats to Cloud Security

The Cloud Security Alliance (CSA), a group of cloud vendors and customers published in March 2010 a white paper discussing the "top threats to cloud computing".
We've summarized them below:

- ▷ **Abuse and nefarious use of cloud computing:** CSA reports that hackers have embedded malicious software into some cloud infrastructures. CSA recommends service providers employ stricter initial registration and validation processes.

- ▷ **Insecure application programming interfaces:** Businesses use APIs to manage and interact with the cloud. However, a weak set of APIs exposes organizations to many security threats.

- ▷ **Malicious insiders:** Large companies initiate background checks on new employees. Why shouldn't you expect the same of your suppliers?

- ▷ **Shared technology vulnerabilities:** Virtualization hypervisors mediate access between multiple operating systems and the service provider's resources. But hypervisors have exhibited flaws that allow guest operating systems to gain inappropriate levels of control.

- ▷ **Data loss/leakage**: Data can be compromised in many ways, such as by corrupted backups or storage on unreliable media. Businesses should demand providers wipe persistent data before releasing it into the pool, and specify backup and retention strategies.

- ▷ **Account, service and traffic hijacking:** Mitigate the risk of unauthorized access to data by prohibiting the sharing of credentials between users and services.

- ▷ **Unknown risk profile:** How well do you understand your cloud supplier's security strategy and procedures? Ask for full disclosure of procedures for patching schedules, employee access to logs and so on.

## Security Differences Between Private and Public Clouds

Public clouds are convenient: customers sign up, specify their requirements and gain immediate service. An internal private cloud requires businesses to create a converged infrastructure to deliver dynamic compute resources.
Businesses directly control the security of their private clouds. They have considerably less control over the security of public clouds. Often, public cloud providers don't detail their security procedures, though customers can choose from a range of pre-defined service level agreements.

## Certifications from Service Providers

In the absence of cloud-specific security and assurance certifications, many cloud providers are getting SAS 70-certified. Developed by the American Institute of Certified Public Accountants (AICPA), this certification verifies the description of a service provider's control processes.

However, the processes are defined by the service provider and not by the AICPA. It's up to the customer to determine whether the controls are adequate.

ISO 27001 is another existing security certification that some cloud providers are adopting. The CSA describes it as a better standard for cloud services than SAS 70. That's because it specifies how service providers should handle security controls and risk assessment. However, like SAS 70, the controls are self-defined.

In March 2010, CSA announced the development of a vendor-neutral "Trusted Security Certification" program. It is aimed at helping cloud providers develop industry-recommended, secure and interoperable identity, access and compliance management practices. CSA will incorporate reference models and certification criteria from existing standards and aims to complete the project in 2010.

### How Can Service Providers Ensure Cloud Security?

The buzz at the 2010 RSA Conference was business concern over the cloud security that service providers offer. That's compounded by the CSA's top cloud threats report warning that some cloud services have unwittingly hosted malicious software. One of the speakers at RSA said businesses would feel reassured if providers could demonstrate effective policy enforcement, prove compliance and manage multi-tenancy.

> Gone will be the day where specific business units "owned" their servers and applications

Service providers should seek solutions that offer increased vulnerability assessment, enhanced data protection and improved compliance controls. A common reference model, such as HP's "Security, Compliance and Continuity Services", can help clients manage cloud security risks. Security issues addressed include applications, business continuity, data integrity, data center and risk management.

## 9.8.    Private or Public Cloud? What Matters and When

We have described several cloud scenarios – but cloud 2 and 3 are the most relevant here. Cloud 2 is essentially the basis for private cloud or internal cloud – delivering IT or applications as a service to internal users only – and the critical activity making this a cloud offering and not simply a utility computing offering is the ability to recognize who used what, when – and then charge for it – either through a formal pricing and recovery mechanism, or simply internal accounting. It drives accountability at all levels, because the consumer or internal customer can now clearly understand the financial impact of requesting that service, and the IT organization understands clearly what it costs to deliver and support it according to an agreed service level agreement – and any changes needed to meet a new business need are very rapidly communicated, implemented, and delivered – within hours typically!

Public cloud or cloud 3 will accelerate in adoption and become so prolific it will become a commonplace means of accessing IT services, but today is really the domain of specific providers – telecommunications companies, Internet service providers because they provide a more generic offering – perhaps at a perceptively lower cost, but with lower or no SLAs, little or no organizational customization and all the inherent security issues accompanying data in an essentially public domain.Using cloud-based infrastructure services doesn't always mean sending your precious data to a third-party provider. While services such as Amazon EC2 are great for SMBs or enterprises with occasional workload spikes, sometimes organizations want the benefits of a cloud with more control, flexibility and security assurances than a third party can provide.

That's why some companies looking to adopt a shared-services operating model are choosing to build their own internal clouds. Here we cover the differences between internal and public clouds, what an internal cloud can do for your organization, and what you should do to prepare for building your own.

| Internal cloud vs. public cloud | | |
|---|---|---|
| **Characteristic** | **Internal cloud** | **Public cloud** |
| Highly scalable | Yes | Yes |
| Fast service rollout | Yes | Yes |
| Security | Behind company firewall | Must rely on vendor security |
| Architecture | Single tenant | Multi-tenant |
| Capital expense | Yes; company must buy hardware | No; vendor owns hardware |
| Operating expense | Infrastructure operating costs | Pay-per-use billing |

When most people think of cloud computing, they think of the most visible examples, such as Amazon EC2, Google AppEngine and Microsoft Azure. Those services are public clouds, which means they operate outside of customers' firewalls. The resources that power the clouds are owned by the companies that operate them, not by the customers.

Perhaps the biggest feature of public clouds is they give customers a way to avoid purchasing and managing certain hardware and software. That's why they're so attractive to organizations that don't have the budget or internal resources to make this capital expenditure.

> Companies can create new revenue streams by offering the internal cloud to external companies

An internal cloud, on the other hand, is owned by the company and operates behind the company firewall. An internal cloud doesn't let companies ditch hardware altogether. Instead, it's all about creating dynamically available resources based on a highly virtualized, tightly integrated, converged infrastructure.

## What's the Better Model?

Both internal and public clouds can be excellent choices, depending on a company's unique requirements. But internal clouds are becoming popular because they offer a degree of flexibility, compliance, security, transparency and control that public clouds typically don't.

### Public cloud: easy start up, less control

To understand the benefits of internal clouds, let's first look at the advantages and disadvantages of public clouds. On the plus side, public clouds are convenient and easy to use. The infrastructure is already set up, so you don't have to worry about how to build it. You simply go to the provider's web site, order a service, and pay for only what you use.

On the other hand, public clouds don't afford the control that customers have within their own firewalls. That means the provider may not use the exact security, privacy, and compliance mechanisms that your business requires. Although you can choose from a menu of services and service level agreements (SLA), your pricing options are limited. The biggest worry, however, is that everything that could go wrong is out of your hands.

## Internal cloud: more control, more service delivery options

An internal cloud is an attractive alternative because it features many benefits of public clouds without any of the drawbacks. Your organization can stick to its tried-and-true security mechanisms. You can maintain specific compliance procedures that might be required for your industry. You can maintain the benefits of the IT infrastructure you've already built. You can fine-tune every part of your internal cloud without feeling beholden to a third-party.

Another benefit of internal clouds: companies can create new revenue streams by offering the internal cloud to external companies – in the Financial Services Industry we expect areas of deep organizational competence to be a key focus area for this growth without giving away any competitive advantage – you might provide a platform for others to use on a billable basis with accompanying SLAs – it is how that platform is used that creates the competitive advantage, not necessarily the platform itself.

One drawback is that, depending on an IT organization's maturity and existing infrastructure, building an internal cloud may call for additional capital and skills. But for many companies, the ability to serve multiple BUs and fulfill multiple SLAs quickly and consistently provides plenty of justification for the immediate expense.

# Datacenter Management and Virtualization

Contribution: Microsoft

This chapter is based on the white paper
Datacenter Management and Virtualization,
published by Microsoft Corporation,
June 2010

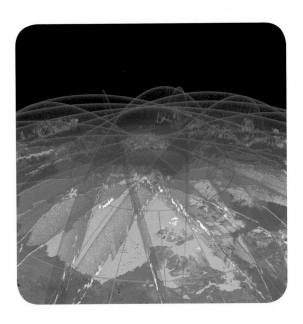

# 10. Datacenter Management and Virtualization

## 10.1. Executive Overview

This chapter is more technical than most of the others. In this article Microsoft focuses on their own Datacenter Services solution. The solution encompasses three scenarios that progress IT infrastructure services from a basic level, through standardized and rationalized, and finally to a holistic, dynamic datacenter solution.

This allows businesses to effectively deliver IaaS within their organization. Each offering stage is designed to be comprehensive and includes infrastructure, management, security, operations, support guidance, software, and processes that will allow enterprise organizations to evolve their datacenters in a controlled and predictable way.

A well-planned transition to the cloud with datacenter management and virtualization technologies will help IT organizations provide reliable datacenter services, improve operational efficiency and enable deeper alignment with business objectives to transform their datacenters into a strategic IT asset.

## 10.2. Customer Challenges in the Datacenter

Driven by the ever-present business needs to control costs, streamline operations, and improve organizational agility, many IT-organizations have been attempting to optimize their datacenter services and derive more value out of their existing investments. Datacenter infrastructure and applications are increasingly being virtualized rather than being deployed on physical hardware. Further the industry is going through a transition to the potentially transformative trend of cloud computing that offers even greater opportunities to increase agility and reduce datacenter costs.

Today's IT organizations face many serious datacenter challenges, including:

> **Delivery of reliable services.** This is the core challenge for IT organizations: they need to deliver highly available services in a reliable and predictable manner. Datacenters are becoming increasingly heterogeneous and globally distributed, requiring IT managers to have a holistic, operational view across all their datacenter environments.

> **Operational efficiency.** With constant operational budget pressures, datacenter virtualization is often considered a key way to reduce costs. However, many organizations that have virtualized still struggle with escalating datacenter costs and datacenter complexity. For instance, virtual servers are often added to an ever-increasing landscape of virtual-server sprawl without any improvements in IT management and process flow. Additionally, compliance costs continue to rise due to increased regulatory pressures. This illustrates the need for simplified and automated processes combined with centralized management.

> **Improved business responsiveness.** In today's dynamic business environment, there is a lot of pressure on IT to be agile and responsive to changing business needs. This has implications in terms of building flexible and elastic IT capabilities to match IT capacity with business demand. In response, IT organizations have started to investigate cloud solutions. However, many are unsure of how and where to begin making such a transition.

## 10.3. Datacenters Evolving to Cloud Computing: Management is Key

Many organizations have implemented virtualization initiatives and are seeing benefits like improved utilization, reduced floor space, reduced datacenter management and virtualization power costs, and more. Microsoft sees private-cloud and public-cloud computing as the next logical step in datacenter optimization with the key driver being improved agility and business responsiveness. (See Figure 10.1) Microsoft defines cloud computing as the ability to deliver IT as a standardized service, allowing IT managers to focus on areas where they can deliver increased business value and efficiency. The term 'private cloud' is used when organizations enable their own cloud-computing capabilities on premises or via dedicated hardware from a third-party hoster. The term 'public cloud' is defined as shared external computing resources hosted by third-party service providers.

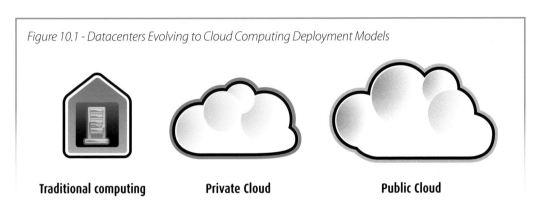

*Figure 10.1 - Datacenters Evolving to Cloud Computing Deployment Models*

**Traditional computing**      **Private Cloud**      **Public Cloud**

Ultimately, many organizations will function with a hybrid model, taking advantage of the benefits offered by both private and public clouds with the flexibility between using on-premises and partner datacenters. In this new kind of datacenter, common management will be critical to ensure IT organizations have holistic visibility into the performance, health, and availability of their datacenter services across physical, virtual, and cloud-based models. To effectively manage the complexity that may result from a hybrid datacenter model and to realize the full benefits thereof, process simplification and automation will also be crucial.

For the past several years, Microsoft has helped enterprise customers to mature their datacenter management and virtualization services and work toward the vision of 'dynamic IT'. Using the Core Infrastructure Optimization (Core IO) model, Microsoft has helped customers progress from a mostly manual, or 'basic', infrastructure to one that's automated and aligned with the business, or which is referred to as 'dynamic'. During this journey, Microsoft has delivered key dynamic-IT tenets, like unified management across physical and virtual environments, model-driven management, and service-focused management. Cloud computing builds on these tenets to deliver compelling agility and cost benefits.

Based on experience running large-scale cloud services like Bing, Windows Live and Windows Azure, Microsoft believes cloud computing has the potential to unlock transformative agility and cost benefits across the full computing stack. Microsoft intends to bring these findings to enterprise datacenters through System Center product capabilities, so businesses can benefit from the Microsoft experience and expertise.

## 10.4. Bridging the Gap Between Private and Public Clouds with Common Management

Microsoft will enable customers to accelerate their transition to cloud computing with its 'server' and 'services' platforms. The server platform, comprised of technologies like Windows Server and System Center, will enable customers and partners (e.g. hosting service providers) to build customized public-cloud and private-cloud solutions in their datacenters, thus continuing to build on existing investments. Windows Azure provides the services platform and will help customers and partners leverage the power of standardized and turnkey cloud-computing solutions.

Regardless of whose datacenter is used for hosting, Microsoft can help bridge the gap between private and public clouds across the whole stack, from infrastructure to applications, with common management, identity, security, and development models.

As can be seen in Figure 10.2, IT is enabled to choose hybrid deployment models based on business requirements and ease of management across multiple environments, finding flexibility without added complexity. 'Service-centric' management is a key tenet to help realize this vision. Service centricity involves holistic management of the service across the lifecycle of the service, including design, composition, deployment, configuration, monitoring, and data protection, regardless of whether the service will be deployed in private-cloud or public-cloud environments. Technologies like application virtualization, automation, and model-driven management enable this vision.

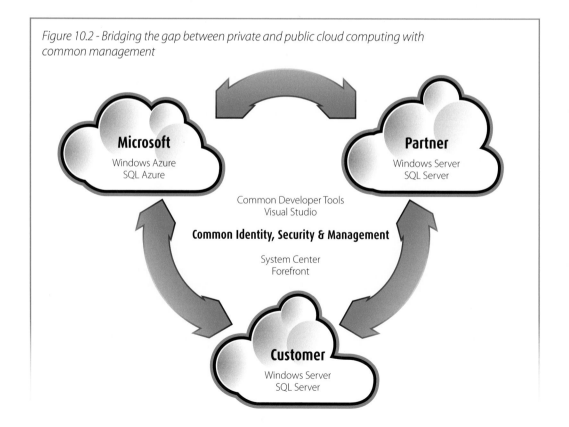

*Figure 10.2 - Bridging the gap between private and public cloud computing with common management*

As an example of common management models across private and public clouds, organizations will soon be able to manage services distributed across on-premises and Windows Azure environments using an on-premises System Center `single pane of glass' console.

## Prepare for Cloud Computing Today

To prepare for cloud computing today, organizations can build on existing investments in Microsoft technologies in the following ways:

- ▣ **Scale virtualization and management across the datacenter**, including business-critical production applications and workloads. This will enable you to focus on optimizing your applications and services in preparation for flexible deployments in hybrid private or public cloud computing models.

- ▣ **Plan for common infrastructure-to-application management** across physical, virtual, and cloud environments to enable holistic operational views across datacenter services.

- ▣ **Standardize and automate datacenter management processes,** starting with simplifying service management processes based on industry standard models, like the Information Technology Infrastructure Library (ITIL) and the Microsoft Operations Framework (MOF), followed by automation to drive down costs and reduce complexity. Deep automation is essential to realizing the full benefits of cloud models.

- ▣ **Have homogeneous resource pools**, as much as possible, to gain the efficiencies of scale that hardware virtualization can offer in cloud environments.

- ▣ **Architect cloud optimized services** that are loosely coupled from the underlying infrastructure.

> Deep automation is essential to realizing the full benefits of cloud models.

## 10.5. Datacenter Management and Virtualization Solutions

The following three Microsoft Datacenter Management and Virtualization solutions are key to helping enterprise organizations transition to cloud-computing.

*Figure 10.3*

| Prepare for Cloud Computing Today | | |
|---|---|---|
| 1 | 2 | 3 |
| Optimize Service Delivery for Datacenter Infrastructure and Business-critical Services | Automate datacenter management processes and support change and compliance | Deliver on-premises private Cloud Computing Foundation |

Let's go over them in turn.

## Optimize Service Delivery for Datacenter Infrastructure and Business-critical Services

Enterprise organizations can deliver reliable datacenter services with optimized virtualization management:

- ▷ Reduce datacenter complexity with integrated, end-to-end management across heterogeneous environments.

- ▷ Create flexible, high-performance virtualization and management for business-critical applications.

- ▷ Optimize datacenter service reliability with cross-site business continuity and disaster recovery.

The above, combined with partner solutions, enable System Center to manage the whole stack, from infrastructure to applications, and to support and manage a breadth of Microsoft and non-Microsoft platforms, tools and applications.

## Automate Datacenter Management Processes and Support Change and Compliance

Enterprise organizations can improve operational efficiency by standardizing and automating datacenter processes in the following ways:

- ▷ **Reduce support costs and improve reliability with integrated service management processes.**
  System Center allows you to streamline datacenter management processes, like incident management, change management, problem management, and more, by implementing industry-standard best practices, like MOF and ITIL, in the form of integrated service management workflows and systems, like the Configuration Management Database (CMDB). This results in lowered operational costs and greater predictability in service delivery.

- ▷ **Lower costs with orchestrated automation of repetitive run-book processes.**
  Automating repetitive processes saves costs, reduces manual errors, and ensures repeatability in process execution. More importantly, it ensures scarce IT resources can focus their time on higher value-added activities. System Center automates workflows in an orchestrated manner between cross-silo processes, systems, and management tools.

- ▷ **Automate enforcement of risk management and compliance using packaged knowledge.**
  System Center enables organizations to demonstrate compliance with key industry regulations and standards by helping streamline end-to-end processes like establishing control objectives, automating implementation of control activities, and fulfilling audit requirements.

- ▷ **Lower costs by automating server lifecycle management.**
  System Center automates server management using in-depth packaged knowledge and policies.

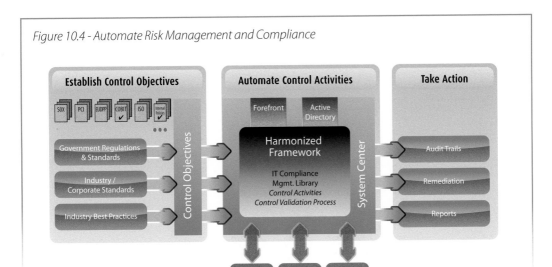

Figure 10.4 - Automate Risk Management and Compliance

## Deliver On-Premises Private Cloud Computing Foundation

The Microsoft Server platform comprised of Windows Server Hyper-V and System Center can enable IT organizations to improve business responsiveness. This is accomplished by delivering on premises cloud computing infrastructure:

- ▷ **On-premises private Cloud Computing** with pooled, shared infrastructure
- ▷ **Enhancing business agility** with self-service IT.
- ▷ **Packaged guidance and best practices** to plan and design dynamic datacenter infrastructure.

In this solution, the VM Manager Self-Service Portal enables enterprises to leverage their existing investments in the Microsoft infrastructure platform, while maturing their IT capabilities to assume advanced cloud capabilities.
The Self-Service Portal is a free, extensible solution that empowers datacenter administrators to dynamically pool, allocate, and manage resources to enable cloud computing on premises. Using this solution, IT organizations create agile, virtualized infrastructures and facilitate business agility, operational efficiencies, and reduced management complexity.

## 10.6. Microsoft Services Can Help Deliver Optimized, Cloud-Ready Datacenters

A well-planned transition to the cloud with datacenter management and virtualization technologies from Microsoft will help IT organizations provide reliable datacenter services, improve operational efficiency and enable deeper alignment with business objectives.
The Datacenter Services solution from Microsoft Services enables organizations to reduce costs, improve operational efficiencies, and drive business agility. The solution encompasses three scenarios that progress IT infrastructure services from a basic level, through standardized and rationalized, and finally to a holistic, dynamic datacenter solution. This allows businesses to effectively deliver IaaS within their organization.

Each offering stage is designed to be comprehensive and includes infrastructure, management, security, operations, support guidance, software, and processes that will allow enterprise organizations to evolve their datacenters in a controlled and predictable way.

Get Ready for Cloud Computing

# Part III
# Case Stories

# Journey to the Private Cloud

A practitioner's guide from EMC's IT department

Contribution: EMC
Customer: EMC
Industry: IT
Solution: virtualization, private cloud

This chapter is based on EMC's white paper "EMC IT's Journey to the Private Cloud".

*To be found on EMC's website*

# 11. Journey to the Private Cloud

A practitioner's guide from EMC's IT department

## 11.1. Executive Overview

EMC, a leading developer and provider of information infrastructure technology and solutions, has a large, internal IT organization that supports the business operations of its global workforce. EMC IT supports more than 48,000 users across over 80 countries and in excess of 400 business applications. Like all IT organizations, EMC IT faces the challenge of balancing cost, risk, and agility in its operations. EMC IT must also justify all of its investments with strong, metrics-based business cases that demonstrate return on investment (ROI) and total cost of ownership (TCO) before receiving management approvals.

### Business need

EMC is transforming its IT operations to improve its customer focus, create business transformation, and deliver operational efficiencies.

### Solution

EMC IT has embraced the private cloud approach to IT infrastructure. By transitioning to a private cloud-based IT infrastructure, and using the advanced capabilities that such an infrastructure provides, EMC IT's ultimate goal is to enable end-to-end, on-demand self-service provisioning of IT services to its customers - the business units at EMC.
EMC IT has been concentrating first on its internal infrastructure to prepare for the transition to the cloud - and virtualization is at the core of this effort in shaping the new infrastructure. There are six key programs. Each initiative's goal is to move the company further along on the process to build integrated infrastructures for virtualization at scale.
In parallel, EMC IT is developing policies and governance mechanisms for managing the new IT services paradigm. The structured approach helps accelerate the journey to the private cloud by enabling the organization to get started with cloud initiatives versus waiting for complete solutions to emerge.

### Benefits

All told, EMC's journey from 2004 through 2009 resulted in savings of $104.5 million, including an estimated $88.3 million in capital equipment cost avoidance and $16.2 million of operating cost reduction due to increased data center power, cooling, and space efficiency. In addition, EMC expects to increase its storage utilization rate from 68 percent to 80 percent and avoid the purchase of more than 1.5 petabytes of storage over five years.

## 11.2. Principles and Priorities

EMC IT's vision is based on three guiding principles: operational efficiency, business transformation, and customer focus.

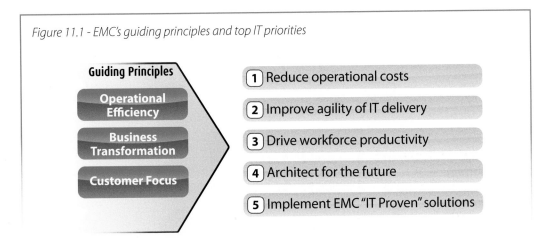

Figure 11.1 - EMC's guiding principles and top IT priorities

## 11.3. A Cloud Computing Strategy: Key to Realizing IT Priorities

EMC IT has embarked on a mission to move to a private cloud-based infrastructure. We define the private cloud as the next-generation IT infrastructure that provides all of the benefits of cloud-based IT systems even as it retains complete control of the IT infrastructure. A private cloud may use internal resources (internal cloud), external resources (external cloud, delivered via service providers in the public cloud), or a combination of both.
Cloud computing has a few differentiating characteristics:

- ☒ IT is built differently using pooled architectures with defined service catalogs for each IT service and the ability to partition/move workloads to where they can best run.

- ☒ IT is run differently by using low- and zero-touch modes for IT operations, provisioning, and management.

- ☒ IT is consumed differently where end consumers of IT services can benefit from on-demand provisioning of IT, based on immediate requirements, and from multiple IT service providers.

- ☒ IT is governed differently from QoS for services to security as new sets of rules and roles emerge.

Transitioning to a cloud-based model provides the IT organization with the benefits of flexibility, efficiency, and dynamic, on-demand resource allocation. However, the IT organization may need to divest some of the control and choice of IT components to a third-party provider of cloud services, if external service providers are involved.

> EMC believes that the capabilities of the private cloud will first evolve in the internal cloud and then federate out into the external and partner clouds

It is in this context that EMC's governance model in the cloud environment becomes more significant.

EMC believes that the capabilities of the private cloud will first evolve in the internal cloud and then federate out into the external and partner clouds. The private cloud has to integrate with the public cloud (for example, Salesforce.com).

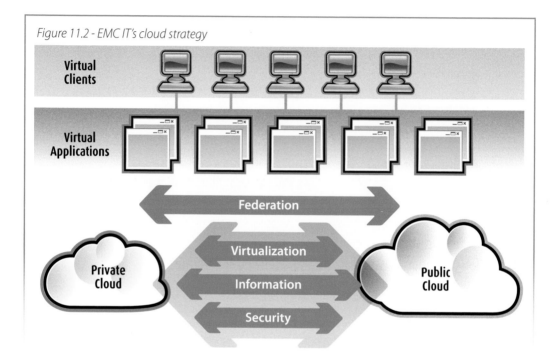

*Figure 11.2 - EMC IT's cloud strategy*

## 11.4. Evolution in the Journey

The internal data center is at the core of the private cloud. Virtualization is the key enabling technology. The evolution to the cloud begins by using virtualization effectively across all components of the data center infrastructure, namely systems, storage, network, security, monitoring and management, the application stack - all the way up to the desktop. Figure 11.3 illustrates this evolution, which involves redefining the IT organization's mandate from being a provider of stand-alone components to being a provider of fully integrated, tested, validated, and ready-to-grow infrastructure and application packages that contain best-in-class components for a data center. The platform adopted is based on the x86 architecture, with 100 percent virtualization leveraging VMware vSphere. The end goal of the transition to the private cloud is to achieve the ability to offer IT as a service to internal customers - the business units at EMC - with options for self-provisioning through a portal interface.

In this model, IT is more than a supplier - IT becomes a business partner - and both IT and the business benefit. With access to IT as a service, the business benefits from the following:

- Simplicity of self-service access

- Alignment of costs with utility with a pay-for-use utility model

- Agility for faster time-to-market and the flexibility to change

- A user-centric, outcome-based approach to supporting business goals

The benefits for IT include efficiency through automation of tasks to do more faster; elasticity to acquire, deploy, change, or release on-demand; greater visibility into costs and control over service levels for better responsiveness; and greater control over the IT environment.

EMC IT is starting to offer services at various levels:

- **Infrastructure as a Service (IaaS)** offers EMC business units the ability to provision infrastructure components such as network, storage, compute, and operating systems as a service.

- **Platform as a Service (PaaS)** provides the application and information frameworks on top of application server, web server, and database components as a service to business units from which to develop solutions.

- **Software as a Service (SaaS)** provides applications and tools in a services model for business enablement.

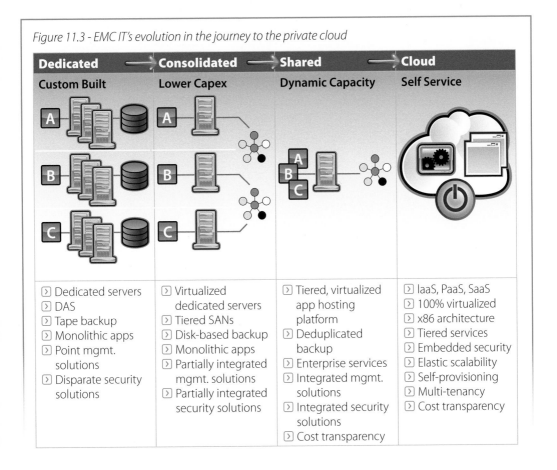

Figure 11.3 - EMC IT's evolution in the journey to the private cloud

| Dedicated → | Consolidated → | Shared → | Cloud |
|---|---|---|---|
| **Custom Built** | **Lower Capex** | **Dynamic Capacity** | **Self Service** |
| - Dedicated servers<br>- DAS<br>- Tape backup<br>- Monolithic apps<br>- Point mgmt. solutions<br>- Disparate security solutions | - Virtualized dedicated servers<br>- Tiered SANs<br>- Disk-based backup<br>- Monolithic apps<br>- Partially integrated mgmt. solutions<br>- Partially integrated security solutions | - Tiered, virtualized app hosting platform<br>- Deduplicated backup<br>- Enterprise services<br>- Integrated mgmt. solutions<br>- Integrated security solutions<br>- Cost transparency | - IaaS, PaaS, SaaS<br>- 100% virtualized<br>- x86 architecture<br>- Tiered services<br>- Embedded security<br>- Elastic scalability<br>- Self-provisioning<br>- Multi-tenancy<br>- Cost transparency |

The next step in the journey is the ability to achieve federation of data and resources between data centers, beginning with internal virtual data centers and going on to federation between internal and external clouds. The aim is to equip the IT organization with the capabilities to move data and resources between internal and third-party data centers to achieve the real benefits of elastic IT provisioning. EMC IT recommends that to manage the progression shown in the previous figure, it is necessary to set up a roadmap, as shown in figure 11.4, that further develops the components of the ecosystem.

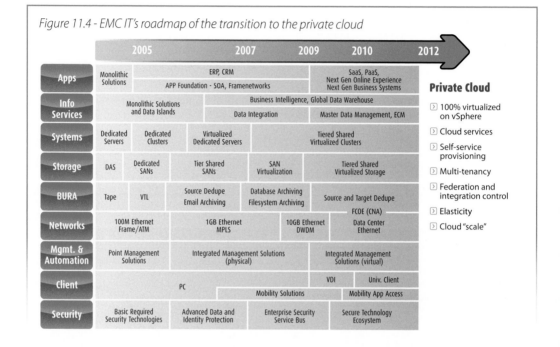

Figure 11.4 - EMC IT's roadmap of the transition to the private cloud

**Private Cloud**

▷ 100% virtualized on vSphere

▷ Cloud services

▷ Self-service provisioning

▷ Multi-tenancy

▷ Federation and integration control

▷ Elasticity

▷ Cloud "scale"

## 11.5. Planning the Transition to the Cloud

In order to transform the IT organization, it isn't enough to just concentrate on changing the technology aspects. An IT transformation initiative must address five perspectives:

▷ Technology

▷ Business capabilities and experience

▷ People

▷ Operations

▷ IT policies/process/governance

Moreover, it is essential not to just consider these elements in isolation but to assess and plan for the complex interactions among them. In line with the components of an IT transformation initiative, EMC believes there are essentially three stages of adoption for organizations that are considering a private cloud strategy at the enterprise level and are at various stages. They are as follows:

▷ The IT Production stage, which targets dev/test/IT applications for virtualization to achieve cost efficiencies. Key capabilities leveraged include shared resource pools and elastic capacity.

▷ The Business Production stage, which enables business applications, including mission-critical applications with an emphasis on high QoS. Key capabilities leveraged include a zero-touch infrastructure and increased control combined with service assurance.

▷ The IT-as-a-Service stage, which emphasizes business agility. Key capabilities include service definition, service catalog, self-service, and chargeback.

Each stage is characterized by business drivers and triggers, level of sponsorship for virtualization, types of applications virtualized, percentage of the x86 server infrastructure virtualized, and the IT competencies acquired along the journey. Success is measured by tracking business value realized (the value path).

## Step 1: Build the Foundation

As a first step, EMC has been working on building the foundations at the technical level. This involves reaching out to technology practitioners in the IT organization to share information on basic cloud enabling technologies, their operations, and their integration methodologies. As virtualization is a key enabler of the transition to a cloud-based infrastructure, it is critical that IT practitioners learn and understand the impact of applying virtualization. Given the rapid pace of technology developments and extensions in the areas of virtualization and cloud computing, it is important that these discussions cover the current state of technology as well as trends, scenarios, and alternatives that might emerge in this vibrant segment of the IT landscape.

It is also critical to encourage technologists to look beyond individual pieces of the technology and look toward an integrated view of how the various components work together. This requires investments in hiring and cultivating specialists who can provide an overall view.

## Step 2: Accelerate Change

The next step consists of bringing discussions to the operations level with the delivery audience - those people focused on delivering IT services to the business. These discussions should focus on the two clear agendas of IT operations personnel:

▷ Leveraging new technologies to better meet key performance indicators used to measure IT effectiveness.

▷ Making organizational and process changes, including the policy and governance mechanisms needed, to fully leverage the capabilities of the new technologies.

Changes in technology can provide only limited benefits to businesses unless accompanied by process and organizational change. Therefore, challenging standard operating procedures, default assumptions around service levels and IT provisioning, and even the way IT is accounted and paid for, are essential to these discussions. These conversations may also result in the development of new operational roles, metrics, and service delivery models patterned around the concept of delivering IT as a service. However, during discussions at this level, EMC has found that it is critical to recognize the close links between people and processes, and pay careful attention to the complex interplays between operations, processes, and organizational change.

## Step 3: Focus on the Advantages of Service Management

Business units may not fully understand the advantages in migrating to a private cloud-based IT infrastructure beyond IT cost reduction. Therefore, EMC IT discovered that it is critical to educate businesses leaders about the additional value that EMC IT can create for them by leveraging the benefits of the cloud infrastructure. Discussions with business units must focus on the enhanced service management benefits the new infrastructure offers, such as:

⊡ Introducing new services that can drive value to business units (for example, truly elastic IT provisioning, choice of service providers, and utility chargeback models).

⊡ Reducing the cycle time for businesses through self-service IT provisioning, choice of multiple providers, and service level agreement-based IT service delivery.

⊡ Providing customers, clients, and employees with better user experiences through optimized IT infrastructures.

EMC IT recognizes that an important transformational initiative of this nature brings with it the need for organizational change as well as a change in behavior from its employees. Continuous education and communication are crucial to getting the organization ready for this journey.

## 11.6. Building a Private Cloud Infrastructure

At the heart of the transition to the private cloud is EMC IT's "Virtualize Everything" strategy, which focuses on virtualizing all elements of a data center: systems, storage, network, security, monitoring and management, application stack (applications, databases, middleware), and even the desktop.

EMC IT identified six key programs along with a use case (virtual desktop), referenced in figure 11.5 and described next, to make the transition to a private cloud-based IT organization.

*Figure 11.5 - Key programs leading to private cloud*

| | Program | Key Technologies |
|---|---|---|
| 1 | Server Virtualization and Consolidation | vSphere, Vblock, VCE with Avamar |
| 2 | Optimized Storage and Network Virtualization | Symmetrix VMAX, SAN virtualization, PowerPath/VE, FAST, VP LEX |
| 3 | Backup and Recovery | Avamar, Data Domain |
| 4 | Security | RSA Authentication Manager, DLP, and Federated Identity Manager, and Archer |
| 5 | Management and Automation | Ionix Unified Infrastructure Manager and SCM, Insight, CapacityIQ, SRM |
| 6 | Applications and Cloud Experience | SpringSource, vCloud, Atmos |
| 7 | Virtual Desktop | View 4.0, RSA, Vblock |

## 1. Server Virtualization and Consolidation

EMC IT started on a server virtualization and consolidation exercise across all of its enterprise data centers. By 2008, 1,250 servers were consolidated into just 250 machines, a transition that has reduced space requirements by 60 percent and power and cooling costs by 70 percent. By ensuring that all new solutions are VMware-compliant, and by following an aggressive plan to consolidate 1,600 additional servers to 40 servers over 2009-2010, EMC expects to save $13 million in costs and save an additional $10 million over the next five years, as well as dramatically reduce its carbon footprint and improve CPU and memory utilization rates.

## 2. Optimized Storage and Network

By leveraging EMC's own experience and product portfolio in the storage and information lifecycle management (ILM) space, the IT department is working on further optimizing information storage for a cloud-based storage design. EMC IT has moved to a five-tier configuration from a two-tier storage model and has also increased the utilization of its storage infrastructure by 19 percent.
EMC expects to increase its storage utilization rate from 68 percent to 80 percent, thereby avoiding the purchase of more than 1.5 petabytes of storage over five years. EMC expects to achieve the goal of 100 percent virtualized storage by 2011.

## 3. Backup, Recovery, and Archiving

By using EMC solutions for replication, backup, recovery, and archiving, EMC facilitates highly effective information management from a virtual cloud-based infrastructure. In addition, data deduplication capabilities increase the efficiency of the backup-to-disk policy. Key benefits include reducing overall backup by 50 percent; decreasing backup time by 75 percent.

## 4. Security

A private cloud perspective involves the ability for IT managers to freely move and federate data and resources across internal and external clouds. Therefore, it is critical to enhance security to support multi-tenancy; data leakage protection; governance, risk, and compliance (GRC); and carrier security requirements. EMC collaborates with divisions such as RSA and Archer to virtualize security components and develop governance, risk, and compliance tools to monitor and manage the challenges related to transitioning IT to a private cloud-based infrastructure.

## 5. Management and Automation

As private cloud-based IT management becomes a reality, it is imperative to track IT resources and information using an integrated tool suite. EMC's Ionix suite of IT management software provides a single-pane-of-glass view of all of the IT resources across the virtualized data center. Using the advanced integrated IT management capabilities of Ionix tools and virtualization management tools from the VMware family EMC IT is working on solutions to accelerate self-provisioning of  IT services, reduce time-to-market, and support innovative chargeback models.

### 6. Applications and Cloud Experience

EMC's vision for the virtualized data center and the transition to the private cloud is to enable its IT organization to offer platforms and applications as services (for example, IaaS, SaaS, and PaaS). EMC is moving application servers, databases, and middleware to a virtualized platform, with the goal to provide them as on-demand infrastructure services to business units for their development activities. And EMC IT has been on the path to providing database grids on Oracle and Microsoft SQL Server to enable virtualized functionality. EMC is working on enabling infrastructures to provide IT in a self-service model to its business units. In addition, EMC IT is planning to use the internal platform to offer compute and storage solutions as a public cloud service to its customers.

### 7. Virtual Desktop Infrastructure - an Implementation Use Case

EMC is working on desktop virtualization approaches to simplify and lower the cost of IT management, increase IT security, optimize information storage, and provision IT resources based on the needs, requirements, and profiles of its workers. The goal is to provision the user and not the device, hence the implementation of VDI will provide the ability for IT to enable different devices used by the end user. This would include the usual company-issued desktop or laptop but extend to a bring-your-own-device model in addition to thin clients and mobile devices. EMC plans to have 100 percent virtualized desktops by 2012, resulting in improved and simplified security, lower client TCO, rapid deployment, reduced support costs, and user-based provisioning.

## 11.7. Making the Transition to the Private Cloud

Before transitioning existing IT resources to a private cloud-based infrastructure, EMC IT performs the following key activities.

### Ensure basic enabling technologies work

The first activity is to ensure that the basic enabling technologies work, as advertised. This requires rigorous testing of all infrastructure components within the virtualized data center - compute, storage, network, and orchestration - to ensure that their performance is in line with requirements and established benchmarks.

### Create use cases and assess capabilities across requirements

The second general activity involves creating a high-level framework of use cases within the business and assessing the current capabilities across those requirements. The objective of identifying the use cases is to match the business needs to the appropriate cloud model for providing IT services. The high-level use cases are based on parameters such as time-to-market, demand predictability and IT elasticity, integration needs, network bandwidth and latency, security, risk and compliance, and business impact.

### Define policy and governance mechanisms

The third activity is to define policy and governance mechanisms to manage and operate the private cloud-enabled IT organization. It is essential to define robust mechanisms to handle critical issues around technical characteristics such as security, bandwidth, and integration, followed by performance, which encompasses service delivery aspects such as IT management.

## Private cloud policy and governance framework

The transition to the private cloud directly impacts the revenue, operational and business costs, and risks faced by the organization:

> **Impact to revenue** - The transition to the private cloud helps IT organizations provide improved services to business units. These IT services help business units find new customers, enhance quality while lowering the cost of goods and services delivered, and sell more successfully to existing customers.

> **Impact to costs** - Transitioning the entire IT infrastructure to the private cloud calls for large organizational investments upfront, resulting in significant savings at the end of the transition. Therefore, it is essential to make adequate budgetary provisions initially to receive rewards later.

> **Impact to risks** - A private cloud infrastructure uses both internal and external cloud infrastructures. This calls for new approaches to manage the business and information risks for the organization.

Therefore, it is essential to establish a governance body (involving people from business, finance, legal, and IT disciplines from within the company) for evaluating the migration of IT to a private cloud-based infrastructure.

EMC IT has developed a high-level policy and governance framework to move applications, platforms, and infrastructures to the external and public cloud. EMC has defined lead criteria that decide the policies and governance frameworks for an application:

> **Application classification** - Classifying applications as mission-critical (directly affecting customer service delivery, or affecting EMC's revenue or its reputation), business-critical (critical to the operations of a business unit), or business supporting (a supporting application)

> **Security** - The information security requirements necessary for the application

> **Risk and compliance** - A profile of the risks of incidents, from outages to information leaks, and the required compliance requirements

> **Connectivity** - Bandwidth and performance requirements for globally distributed applications and users

> **Integration** - The requirements to ensure that tightly coupled applications can work together

> **Performance** - Service delivery requirements such as availability, service level agreements, and IT service management

> **Time-to-market** - Rapid provisioning requirements

> **Demand elasticity** - Ability to deal with changes in the requirements of business units, as well as scale-up and scale-down needs

EMC IT has created a set of business use cases, such as those mentioned in figure 11.6, for various profiles of services requested by business units with policies and small-scale governance functions for each use case.

The transition to the private cloud will enable EMC IT with a transparent method for tracking the usage of IT resources by business unit. This empowers EMC IT with the capability of constructing new chargeback models.

Figure 11.6 - A high-level abstraction of EMC IT's policy and governance model for external cloud usage

| Business Unit use cases for Public Cloud | IT Services that will be required to implement Business Unit use case | | | | | | | Policy | Governance mechanism |
|---|---|---|---|---|---|---|---|---|---|
| | Security (Perimeter security, identity mgmt., authentication) | Risk and Compliance assesment | Connectivity (bandwidth, latency) | Integration | Incident response | Management and monitoring | Application classification (mission-critical, business-critical, business) | Confidential data | Joint Review Board |
| Engineering Labs | ✔ | ✔ | ✔ | | | | | | |
| Large non-production workloads | ✔ | ✔ | ✔ | | | | | ⊡ Confidential data ⊡ Connectivity requirements | Risk and Compliance assessment by IT security and network teams |
| Backup, archive, content mgmt., collaboration - latency tolerant apps | ✔ | ✔ | ✔ | ✔ | ✔ | ✔ | ✔ | | |
| Other production BU applications | ✔ | ✔ | ✔ | ✔ | ✔ | ✔ | ✔ | ⊡ Non-mission critical ⊡ Non-business critical | IT Solution Desk process |

## 11.8. Conclusion

EMC's cloud computing strategy is designed to completely transform its IT organization and operations. Such a transformation means making changes in the way IT is built, run, consumed, and governed at the company. The goal of this strategic initiative is to make the IT department a customer-centric provider of end-to-end solutions to meet the business needs of the business units.

Leveraging the power of the private cloud, innovative services are introduced such as on-demand IT infrastructure provisioning and self-service options for IT service enablement.

To facilitate this transition, EMC IT has concentrated its efforts on the definition of a clear strategy for internal cloud implemented through six programs, which focus on transitioning its IT infrastructure to the virtualized data center model.

To prepare the organization for a new paradigm of IT operations, EMC IT is also educating stakeholders at various levels on the new IT service paradigms, as well as developing a strong policy and governance framework for managing the new IT infrastructure. Working closely with partners and product divisions, EMC IT is concentrating on maximizing the business benefits of technology that can move its existing IT infrastructure to the private cloud.

The structured approach helps accelerate the journey to the private cloud. It provides the company with the opportunity to begin cloud initiatives without waiting for complete solutions to emerge even as it moves from the Business Production stage to the IT-as-a-Service stage (figure 11.7). This enables IT to more easily leverage these solutions as technologies evolve.

All told, EMC's journey from 2004 through 2009 resulted in savings of $104.5 million, including an estimated $88.3 million in capital equipment cost avoidance and $16.2 million of operating cost reduction due to increased data center power, cooling, and space efficiency.

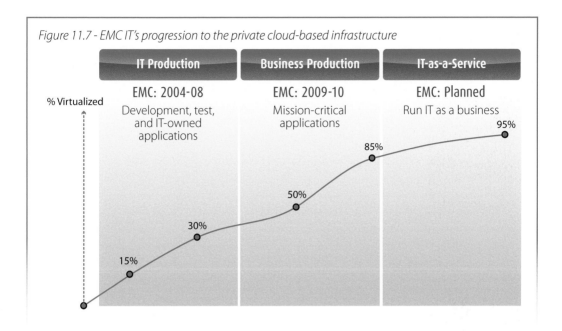

Figure 11.7 - EMC IT's progression to the private cloud-based infrastructure

Looking forward, EMC expects to increase the storage utilization rate from 68 percent to 80 percent and avoid the purchase of more than 1.5 petabytes of storage over five years. By having "risk versus reward" conversations with stakeholders at each level, EMC's IT department has been successful in accelerating the adoption of private cloud-based technologies within the company.

# Virtual Workplaces at Wolters Kluwer

Customer: Wolters Kluwer

Industry: Publishing

Solution: flexible workplaces, thin clients, virtual desktop infrastructure, SharePoint, outsourcing;

Integrator: CSC

# 12. Virtual Workplaces at Wolters Kluwer

## 12.1.  Executive Overview

Kluwer, subsidiary of the global Wolters Kluwer, is an information services and publishing company. It provides products and services for professionals in the health, tax, accounting, corporate, financial services, legal and regulatory sectors.

**Business Need**

In recent years, Kluwer has transformed itself from a traditional publisher to an online publisher. This required automated production and publishing processes, and an integrated user environment. An earlier transition to Server Based Computing (SBC) did not bring the required flexibility. Legacy applications made it difficult to offer the required functionality to employees working on thin clients or at home.

**Solution**

The implementation in the Dutch branch of a Virtual Desktop Interface offered Wolters Kluwer the desired performance and robustness to modernize its application portfolio and workplaces. The number of applications was reduced, as legacy applications were to be phased out. At the same time, Office 2000 and Internet Explorer version 6 were upgraded to Office 2007 and SharePoint was introduced.

**Benefits**

VDI is transparent to the end user. After logging in, the virtual desktop provides the same experience as a traditional PC. This way, Kluwer was able to reduce the number of fat clients by more than ninety percent in less than a year. As a result, the number of laptops was substantially reduced. Employees are now able to perform their work and access information from any location at any time with rich enduser experience.

## 12.2.  Kluwer Lifts its Infrastructure to the Next Level

Two years ago, Kluwer decided to move its Server Based Computing infrastructure to the next level. A Virtual Desktop Infrastructure (VDI) would bring those benefits previous transitions were not fully able to realize. Now that this project has been completed, it appears that users at Kluwer are finally getting the integrated environment they have been waiting for.
In the process, Kluwer has transformed itself into a modern online publisher. "When processing legislative amendments, producing loose-leaf binders or books took weeks or months. As a result, these publications were never really up-to-date." That was no longer acceptable in an online world, says CTO Martin Wuite. "To speed up this process, we had to integrate all steps -- from author to customer -- into the same Kluwer environment."
"Seven years ago, we started standardizing and rationalizing. We reduced the number of applications en introduced flexible workplaces. We outsourced to CSC, including the transfer of 26 out of 50 employees from our IT department. Two years ago, this contract was extended. We wanted to take our infrastructure to the next level, using virtualization and cloud computing, although back then nobody called it the cloud."

## Outsourcing

The first thin clients were deployed in the company almost seven years ago. Back then, Kluwer introduced SBC based on Citrix technology. Previously, the IT department had been outsourced to service provider CSC. "When we adopted this new technology, it was also a natural point to start outsourcing," Wuite says. "Otherwise we would have had to invest a lot in infrastructure and skills."

As envisaged, the transition to SBC would have allowed users to log in to their business applications from any Kluwer office or from home. And, of course, thin clients were less expensive, to purchase, and to maintain.

## Unruly Applications

However, things did not work out as expected. "After five years, we had to conclude that our initial targets had not been reached," Wuite explains. "We aimed to have a ratio of eighty percent thin clients and twenty percent traditional desktop and laptop systems in five years. But two years ago it was only fifty-fifty. This was mainly caused by the fact that we were not able to standardize our applications. At the start of the project that introduced VDI we had over 600 applications in use. Last year, that number was down to about 300. Of those, 226 were virtualized."

"Furthermore, we have a number of legacy applications that cannot be virtualized, and it is too expensive to migrate them. For example, some of our publications are still produced using older Word versions or even WordPerfect. These applications can contain so many macros that we have to leave the old environment as it is. We decide on that for each individual application."

"Even in the new VDI environment, about forty traditional workplaces were kept intact for that reason. So it is true that we did not realize the full business case for the SBC transition. Costs have been decreased substantially, but not as much as we wanted."

## From Corporate to It Strategy

"Every three years, the Kluwer board creates a new business development plan," says Wuite. "The IT department then implements the necessary changes for the IT infrastructure. This has led to the set up of global shared service centers and to changes in the way our infrastructure (i.e. workplaces, data centers and hosting) and back-office (i.e. SAP, Finance, CRM, and HR) are organized."

The latest corporate strategy (2010-2012) rests on three pillars. For us to deliver value at the point-of-use, users should be able to access their applications from any place and at any time. The same goes for the partner networks. Business processes should be integrated into complete value chains. Finally, innovation and effectiveness should be improved by creating so-called global capabilities. Until the beginning of this year, Wolters Kluwer was organized per country. Now, there are four verticals: tax & accounting, legal & regulatory, financial & compliance, and health & pharma.

IT is represented at the highest level of the Kluwer organization. "I am a member of both the Dutch and the global IT management team," Wuite explains. "Every month we discuss on a country level programs and related costs, planning and milestone-dates. On a corporate level the ITLC (IT Leadership Council) agrees on all IT initiatives."

## 12.3. Latest and Greatest

Kluwer completed its transition to VDI in the Netherlands at the beginning of this year. Over a period of one year, almost 700 PCs were replaced by thin clients, allowing most users to work from any workplace at the office and from their own computer at home. Currently, only fourty traditional desktop systems remain at the Kluwer offices at Alphen aan den Rijn, Amsterdam, and Deventer. And these will soon be gone too, as the company is actively phasing out the last legacy applications.

Speed was the most important reason to lift the SBC environment to the next level. "This technology was outdated," Wuite explains. "Most of the editors had to use traditional desktop computers to run heavy applications. When accessed from home, the performance of applications like these was unacceptable. Furthermore, while people were using the latest and greatest software at home, Kluwer was still using Office 2000 and Internet Explorer version 6. So together with the introduction of CSC's Dynamic Desktop, we decided to upgrade Office 2007 and introduce SharePoint."

"Unlike the SBC environment, VDI is transparent to the end user. After logging in, the virtual desktop provides the same rich experience as a traditional PC. It looks and feels like an ordinary Windows system. So, if all applications you need have been virtualized, it automatically will suffice to use just thin client hardware. This way, we were able to reduce the number of fat clients by more than ninety percent in less than a year. Moreover, we reduced some 500 workplaces , thanks to removal of redundant workplaces and reduction in personnel. In total, 80 percent of the remaining desktops were replaced by thin clients."

## Cutting Costs

At the same time, the number of (virtualized) applications has been reduced from 226 to 90. For example, all editors are now using the Woodwing publication system combined with InCopy. "The economic crisis has actually made it easier for us to cut expenses. People are far more aware of costs." According to Wuite, the cost of maintenance for a desktop computer is twice a high and for a laptop four times as high as maintenance for a thin client. At the same time, the number of servers that constitute the backoffice of this solution have been reduced by more than half, from about 230 to 110.

Next to cost reductions, the fact that people are now allowed to work from any location and at any time while using any type of computer hardware and still get the rich enduser experience is another important point. "Some applications could only be used from within the Kluwer network. Apart from a few legacy applications, this no longer the case." Of course, this brings along additional risks. Not with regard to security, since access to the SBC environment was already protected using RSA tokens. "Users having access to sensitive data require more attention. We have made additional arrangements with these employees."

## Portable Status Symbol

As part of the KING project (Kluwer Infrastructure Next Generation), the number of laptops was substantially reduced too. "We cut that by 33 percent," says Wuite. "leaving only 170 laptops. Of course, this led to complaints. Some managers found it hard to let go their laptops, as they were considered status symbols. But we adhere rigidly to our policies. We currently provide laptops only to people in sales and marketing who spend a lot of their time on the road, and to a few employees who travel a lot. Our policy is to provide our users access to their data from any place at any time, even on a plane."

Following strict rules is the only way for the IT department to keep their costs under control. "We provide a Single-Point-Of-Contact (SPOC) to the business for users to order their systems and services. If you want to have a laptop, you have to get your request signed by the director and the person responsible for the cost. We had to put up this barrier because in our company IT costs are carried centrally and not declared to the individual business units. Otherwise, the units earning the most money would spend it like water."

## 12.4. Innovation

In retrospective, looking at the combined transition, two out of the three aims have been reached. "We succeeded in creating flexibility for our users," Wuite elaborates. "Before, anything was possible, and anything happened. But offering an online presence requires you to standardize. So, now we are still flexible, but within boundaries."

The same is true for the professionalism of the IT department. "Our people did not have the skills required to manage the transition to SBC and the operation of the new environment. So we would have had to invest heavily in training and education to get our staff up to par. That why we outsourced to CSC. The investments in our own IT department would have been too high, and maintaining the IT environment does not belong to our core business. So, we decided to have CSC run our infrastructure and part of our application support."

Innovation, however, has always remained a source of concern. "Over the years, we have managed to implement three major changes. The first was the SBC workplace. Then there was the so called KING project, providing a virtualized and standardized environment to the end user. And now we have set up a cycle of fast innovations of which most are cloud solutions that support our motto that innovation must make things 'better, faster and cheaper'. Every quarter we organize an innovation meeting, where we develop and initiate new projects."

"In the Netherlands, the relationship between Kluwer and CSC goes back a long time. As both are large international companies, we used to spend a lot of time waiting for each other. At first CSC could only be engaged after we had gone through full requirements specification. Now, we are working jointly as an integral part of the IT governance model between Kluwer and CSC on multiple levels. But it takes years before you can bring your relationship to this level."

### Virtualized Infrastructure

The VDI solution deployed at Kluwer, the Dynamic Desktop Solution, is based on a product set developed by CSC and its partners. Kluwer provides personalized desktops to its users. Every employee has his or her own desktop and is authorized to install software. The solution also allows working off premise (at home, on the road). Benefits are a more secure environment, a reduced number of end devices, and replacement of most fat clients by thin clients. At the moment, 80 percent of all desktops runs in the central datacenter, and are accessed using a thin client. About half of these virtualized desktops are based on SBC technology, the other half on VDI. Current TCO (Total Cost of Ownership) is 7.5 percent lower than before.

# Hay Group Moves Services to Private Cloud

Contribution: Cisco Systems

Customer: Hay Group

Industry: Consulting

Solution: applications moved to hosted private cloud, Infrastructure as a Service

# 13. Hay Group Moves Services to Private Cloud

## 13.1. Executive Overview

Hay Group is a global management consulting firm specializing in developing talent, organizing people to be more effective, and motivating them to perform at their best. They have 2,600 employees; their home base is Philadelphia, Pennsylvania USA.

### Business need

The firm previously hosted web portals and internal business applications on standalone servers in a managed service provider's data center. Each of Hay Group's six business units that delivered subscription services to customers had its own servers, storage, and networks. Hay Group saw an opportunity to increase client service levels by changing the way it hosted applications. The goal was to provide high availability for customer web portals, while protecting intellectual property.

### Solution

The solution was moving applications to a private cloud hosted by IPR International's ZoneIT cloud.
ZoneIT is a secure multitenant cloud, based on Cisco Unified Computing System™ (UCS). This Infrastructure as a Service (IaaS) includes a robust disaster recovery provision.

### Benefits

It now takes minutes instead of weeks to implement a new service. Furthermore the new cloud solution achieved a 99.999 percent availability.

## 13.2. Business Challenge

> With the new private cloud Hay Group can bring up new web portals for their clients almost immediately.

Hay Group is a global management consulting firm specializing in developing talent, organizing people to be more effective, and motivating them to perform at their best. More than 2,600 employees work in 86 offices in 48 countries, serving clients across private, public, and not-for-profit organizations in every major industry.

More than half of Hay Group's revenues come from customer subscriptions to web portals that offer up-to-date research on reward strategies and benefits, which clients use to maximize employee performance. The firm previously hosted these web portals, as well as its internal business applications, on standalone servers in a managed service provider's data center. Each of Hay Group's six business units that deliver subscription services had its own servers, storage, and networks.

Hay Group saw an opportunity to increase client service levels by changing the way it hosted applications. One reason is that clients count on HR information to be available at a moment's notice, and had become increasingly interested in Hay Group's disaster recovery (DR) capabilities. "To increase our value to clients, we decided to move to a fully virtualized environment that increased reliability and availability," says Robert Butler, Global Chief Information Officer for Hay Group. In addition, the firm wanted to empower business units to quickly introduce new client services, sometimes just for a brief opportunity. "We didn't have that flexibility with the traditional hosting model," Butler says.

Hay Group envisioned a private cloud, where the different business units could share the same infrastructure while keeping their information separate on servers, storage, and the network.

## 13.3. Solution

After evaluating private cloud hosting proposals from five managed service providers, Hay Group selected IPR International. "We proposed building a secure, multi-tenant hosting environment in our two hardened data centers, with automated failover. Hay Group would become our first customer for Infrastructure as a Service," says Michael Emmi, Chief Executive Officer of IPR International.

Hay Group and IPR jointly decided to build the private cloud service on Cisco Unified Computing System (UCS), which combines compute, networking, storage access, and virtualization in a cohesive system managed as a single entity. "The Cisco Nexus 1000V Switch played an important role in our decision because it preserves the security profiles of our various client services as we move them between server blades," says Butler.

Hay Group and IPR collaborated with Cisco Advanced Services and Presidio Networked Solutions to build the private cloud infrastructure in just three months, a week earlier than scheduled. "Hay Group and other customers continue to manage their applications, databases, web site, active directory, and other software applications just as they always have, while IPR provides a highly available, secure multi-tenant environment," Emmi says.

Three Cisco UCS chassis with 24 server blades reside in IPR's production data center in Wilmington, Delaware, and another three are housed in the disaster recovery (DR) facility in Reading, Pennsylvania.

Hay Group moved existing virtual machines and approximately 70 new virtual machines over the network to IPR's private cloud, called ZoneIT. After testing application performance in the production and DR environments and practicing DR failover, Hay Group cut over to the cloud by simply changing the DNS entry. Clients were able to access Hay Group services during the cutover, and afterwards, clients in Europe reported that web portal performance had increased by as much as 80 percent.

All 415 of Hay Group's application servers now reside in the private cloud, including the client web portals, Microsoft Exchange, Microsoft SharePoint, HR systems, financial systems, and file and print services. IPR uses multiple Cisco technologies to keep each tenant's applications and data separate.

> Clients in Europe reported that web portal performance had increased by as much as 80 percent.

## 13.4. Results

### Increased Availability

Hay Group can now offer industry-leading SLAs for availability because the cloud platform is built with completely redundant solutions. And in the event of a data center outage, IPR or Hay Group can quickly fail over applications to the other center without interrupting web access for customers. "During testing, we failed over the entire application environment from the production data center to the DR data center in less than 30 minutes," says Marcia Wasserman, Director of Strategic Accounts for IPR International.

Clients can also continue to access information during routine maintenance. When Hay Group upgrades firmware, for example, an administrator applies a service profile to provision an available blade with a few clicks, temporarily moves the virtual machines there, then moves them back to the upgraded blade. Customers experience no down time.

### Increased Agility

The cloud gives Hay Group greater agility by making it easier to collect, aggregate, stage, and clean data to deliver new services to clients. "We can bring up new web portals for our clients in minutes, compared to weeks when we had to provision standalone servers," says Butler.

### Cost Control

Hay Group now needs fewer servers because the 72 GB RAM on Cisco UCS server blades supports 35 virtual machines, compared to 10 to 15 on the previous platform. What's more, hosting all business units' applications and data in the cloud has enabled Hay Group to provide a DR site for all six business units for about the same cost as building a dedicated DR infrastructure for one business unit.

The firm also saves on cable and switch port costs. Previously, the 36 VMware ESX servers used 216 cables, and the 65 traditional rack-mounted web servers used 324 cables. Now all servers are consolidated onto 24 UCS server blades that connect to the data network and storage area network (SAN) through a single pair of Cisco UCS 6100 Fabric Interconnects using 12 cables. "We consolidated from 540 to 12 cables, a 44-to-1 ratio," says Butler. "The Cisco Interconnect also eliminated the need to purchase additional host bus adapters and fibre channel switches to connect our new virtual machines to the storage area network, reducing costs while simplifying troubleshooting."

## Technical Implementation

The Cisco UCS consists of three chassis at each of IPR's two data centers. The chassis contain a mix of Cisco UCS B200 M1 and B250 M1 blade servers with 72 GB RAM, all using the Intel Xeon 5540 processor. The Cisco UCS and Nexus switches in the two data centers are configured identically. All devices, including the Nexus switches and Cisco Adaptive Security Appliances, are implemented in high-availability pairs, with counterparts in the other building. "Moving applications between the two data centers simply requires changing the DNS and network pointing," says Butler.

IPR built a multi-carrier, geographically diverse, high-speed private fiber network to keep the two data center facilities synchronized within 65 milliseconds. Cisco Application Control Engines provide load balancing for traffic arriving over public networks, directing the traffic through switches and firewalls that IPR configured to Hay Group's specifications.

### Operational Efficiency

The Cisco UCS platform helps IPR efficiently deliver its private cloud service to Hay Group and other customers. "Cisco UCS Manager service profiles create ongoing cost savings with less spare hardware," Wasserman says, "If a blade ever fails, we can use Cisco UCS Manager service profiles to identically configure another available blade with a few clicks."

### Next Steps

Based on the success of this project, Hay Group has made it a corporate policy to move all servers that can be virtualized to the private cloud. The firm is beginning with the 250 physical servers currently hosted in global regional processing centers.

Hay Group is also planning to use the IPR ZoneIT private cloud to host virtual desktops.

Hay Group has made it a corporate policy to move all servers that can be virtualized to the private cloud.

# ING Moves Infrastructure Into the Cloud

Business benefits more important than cost containment

Customer: ING

Industry: Finance

Solution: infrastructure consolidation, application rationalization, cloud computing, VBlocks, Tivoli discovery and provisioning, Virtual Clarity, virtual machine orchestration

# 14. ING Moves Infrastructure into the Cloud

Business benefits more important than cost containment

## 14.1. Executive Overview

ING is a global financial institution headquartered in Amsterdam, currently offering banking, investments, life assurance and retirement services to meet the needs of a broad customer base.

**Business Need**

ING's IT infrastructure in the Benelux is spread across sixteen data centers and server rooms. Decades of computing and mergers has led to a complex, inflexible, and potentially unstable environment.

**Solution**

Current infrastructure is being consolidated into five existing data centers. Then, a second step will be made, concentrating these into two new facilities. At the same time, the number of applications will be reduced.

**Benefits**

While this transition is expected to bring substantial savings in cost and personnel, taking control of the IT infrastructure, refreshing the technology, improving stability, and making the bank more agile are far more important.

## 14.2. Complex infrastructure

ING's Benelux IT infrastructure is spread across sixteen data centers and server rooms all over the Benelux. Historically, back-office applications were not managed by corporate IT. This complex legacy reflects decades of automation, including a series of mergers. With the appointment of a new CIO in 2007, the decision was made to modernize and centralize the infrastructure. The major objectives of this transition are to reduce the bank's risk exposure and to modernize technology to improve the business agility of the bank. Cost containment is seen as an important side effect.

"We have sixteen facilities that we would label as data centers," says Danny O'Connor, head of technology services. "But there are in fact significantly more sites that have systems, and a lot of them are considered production systems. So, there are really a lot of ING locations across the Benelux that needs to be addressed."

"In some cases, we have a legacy of twenty years or more," adds Tony Kerrison, head of infrastructure services. "It has at no time been fully refreshed. Among other considerations, this inheritance is creating instability in the environment."

Like most (financial) organizations, the Internet era forced ING to put most of its IT efforts into adding new capabilities and services to existing systems. "Over the last decade, there has been a lack of investment into infrastructure technology," admits O'Connor. "There has not been significant technology refresh, up to a point where we now have core environments that are no longer supported by the vendor. In a lot of cases, those no longer meet our operational engineering standards of what we consider current and supportable."

"These problems increase the inherent level of risk. As a result, we have had some outages. From a risk perspective, we have to invest more money on addressing our data center issues and on our technology. Risks are obviously there and increasing every year."

## 14.3. Provider of Choice

According to O'Connor, the current situation is partly the result of the bank's success. "Yes, the bank did continue to invest in technology, but predominantly in new functionality and new markets, not in the existing systems."
"ING's IT department is not able at this moment to articulate the benefits of its services to the business. So the business asks me, unless you can offer me an attractive alternative, why should I come to you guys? Our mission and mantra is that we want to be the technology provider of choice for our business. So we want to present our services, our cost, and our service levels in such a way that they want to use us, rather than do it themselves or go to another vendor."

> Tony Kerrison: "We are using virtualization to help improve our efficiency and make better use of our assets."

Kerrison describes the CROQS model ING uses to specify the aims for this transition. "It stands for Cost, Risk, Optionality, Quality of Service (QoS), and Scalability. We should see the cost structure diminish. We are using virtualization to help improve our efficiency and make better use of our assets. If you look at the risks, we will be using standard platforms and standard stacks of technology. That incorporates all of the security and controls the bank needs from a risk perspective. 'Optionality' means that we end up with applications that are mobile. We will use virtualization to move applications seamlessly across various infrastructures."
"This also improves our Quality of Service," Kerrison continues. "It improves the resilience of our services, because we can move applications seamlessly between data centers and across different parts of our infrastructure. Finally, 'scalability' refers to how we can grow or shrink the infrastructure easily, since we are using standardized components of very flexible nature. So, these are the drivers behind our move to new data centers, our move towards virtualization, and ultimately our move towards cloud technologies."

## 14.4. Consolidation

ING has already been through the first phase of the transition to the cloud. "We have moved to virtualization on every platform," says Kerrison. "In the x86 environment, we have over a thousand virtual machines running applications. One hundred percent of our AIX platform has been virtualized. On the Solaris platform, we are moving significant numbers of applications onto Solaris Containers. And our mainframe, obviously, is by definition in a virtualized environment. All this technology we are working with is really cloud-enabling. The final step to the actual cloud will be automated provisioning. And we release that at the beginning of 2011 for the x86 platform using Tivoli Service Automation Manager (TSAM), providing Infrastructure-as-a-Service (IaaS). Over time this will be expanded to Platform-as-a-Service (PaaS)."
Since most of the servers have already been virtualized, moving the machines themselves is the easy part. At this moment, ING is planning the facilities that will eventually host the virtualized infrastructure. "In the medium term, we are going to consolidate the business applications in our data centers in Amsterdam, Rotterdam and Belgium," says Kerrison. "The applications and the office phone system will remain housed locally."
"In the longer term, the two facilities in Amsterdam, the one in Rotterdam, and the two in Belgium will be replaced by two dedicated, purpose-built facilities, probably one in Holland and one in Belgium."

> "In the next couple of years, we will bring this down from 2500 to 1700 applications. And we are aiming at a fifty percent reduction in the long term."

"We are currently in the final phase of deciding how to implement this. We can invest bank capital in those facilities, or we can source from the market in a number of ways. We can have someone build the facilities for us on a wholesale basis and bill us for the monthly costs with a little bit of margin on top. Or we can go for the more traditional retail options where we have a lot more flexibility in terms of contract length, allowing us to be more dynamic. However, this retail flexibility is much more expensive, three of four times the price of doing it ourselves. So we are currently comparing the benefits of investing the bank's capital versus the flexibility we would get from a retail solution. We will decide by the end of this year, and then implement it at the beginning of 2011."

## 14.5. Application Rationalization

Together with the refresh and consolidation of the infrastructure, the number of applications will be reduced too. "Currently, there are 2500 applications out there," says O'Connor, "which is far too many. In the next couple of years, we will bring this down to 1700 applications.

### ING's Infrastructure

"We have mainframes and mid-range systems which we will maintain and continue to operate for the foreseeable future," O'Connor says. "Banking will be relying on some of these systems for some time to come. In the mid-range and open systems space, we have Windows, we have a small Linux section, we have a reasonably large Solaris deployment, and some AIX (IBM UNIX) environments too."

"For the hosting of our x86 systems, we have selected VBlocks from the VCE Coalition, which is an alliance between VMware, Cisco, and EMC. They deliver predictable building blocks providing a virtual x86 environment. In the AIX-space, we are using IBM's latest platform (Power7). And with Sun (now part of Oracle) we are deploying their latest technology, including Solaris 10 containers. Although we use different architectures for the front-end, they are consistently coupled to the EMC main storage at the back-end. We use a Hitachi system as a virtual tape infrastructure, and some physical tape for regulatory or other compliance-type reasons. All systems are managed using IBM's Tivoli suite."

We have some applications that are five years through a twelve year expected life cycle. So, some of these applications will be around for another seven years at least."

"These are just the initial numbers from the first set of plans we put together," Kerrison elaborates. "Currently we are compiling an inventory of our applications, doing an assessment of each individually. At the end of this process, we would expect to see a more significant decrease. We are aiming at a fifty percent reduction in the long term."

"There will always be a certain number of legacy systems driving our over-all costs," says O'Connor. "We will try and differentiate our pricing, obviously. Like I said, we need to make it attractive and be the service provider of choice at the right price. But we will influence people by pricing legacy systems much more expensive."

## 14.6. Constraints and Concerns

Of course, security is the biggest concern for this transition. "Security around our data and clients is critical to our business," says O'Connor. "We need to be extremely aware and sensitive to security issues. Especially issues related to the public and semi-private clouds are the hardest to solve and will take time."

Environmental concerns are another important constraint. "We have of course corporate social responsibility commitments. We measure energy consumption in terms of PUE (Power Usage Effectiveness, a measure for the efficiency of a data center). If you look at a data center built five years ago, it would have a PUE of 2.0. Two years ago, you might have achieved a PUE of 1.6. We will be hitting a low 1.2, which really is industry leading. That is quite amazing, from 2.0 five years ago to 1.2 now. If we were to look at a data center built two years ago compared to what we are intending to build now, that represents a saving of 35,000 tons of $CO_2$ per annum, which also translates into 14 Gigawatts of energy per year."

Alongside all technical changes, ING is putting major effort into redefining IT operations into a set of services. ING is for example moving to a much more self-service oriented model for provisioning of systems. O'Connor: "And that is a big step on the way to a cloud-enabled environment. To make sure we get this right, we have partnered with Virtual Clarity. They bring an external perspective and significant expertise in both executing the change and in modernizing IT operations. Our goal is to provide a framework for robust, nimble and flexible services that our clients will be happy with."

This framework will allow ING to deliver greater efficiency and closer customer integration over time. "We are looking at every aspect of our operating model, from how we align our plans with our clients to how we introduce and operate services, and how we manage end-of-service life."

"The infrastructure we supply is open to the application development teams," Kerrison adds. "So they are able to develop new innovations. For example, rolling out support for mobile and internet communications on a much faster timeline. Scalability, faster time-to-market, and faster use of technology are all very important aspects. Furthermore, as cloud services become more available, we will use these and integrate them into our current application architectures."

In the meantime, Kerrison sees a lot of opportunity for synergies between the business demands and the current transition plans. "Infrastructure is the foundation, supporting the business. As we are looking at strategic data centers and thinking about the technologies we put in there, we have to keep in mind that these are enabling the business. So, the applications build on top of our infrastructure, holding the business logic in it, are ultimately providing products for our customers."

## The Right Tools

ING has a huge, complex infrastructure across multiple locations. IT doesn't know every application and system that is out here. According to O'Connor a tool called TADDM (Tivoli Application Dependency Discovery Manager) will help them discovering all the components of the application infrastructure. "Once deployed, the tool will inform us about the complexity of our existing environment. In an unobtrusive way TADDM will provide a map of our application infrastructure. We need to know what we have on hand before we can move forward."

Another important tool is TSAM (Tivoli Service Automation Manager). "It provides a common front-end for the provisioning -- in modern terms, the services -- for all these platforms, whether it is Windows, Linux, Solaris, or AIX. So an engineer or developer at the business can go to this self-service website and say "I would like an AIX machine of this kind of flavor". These variants are part of our service catalog. This way, we can move to a much more self-service oriented model for provisioning of systems. And that is a big step on the way to a cloud-enabled environment."

"We expect to select another orchestration tool, that would sit on top of TSAM. This would manage the cloud, help us to move workloads inside and outside to a public cloud. Those tools are now emerging but they are still immature. However, we expect them to mature as our needs evolve. Probably in a year's time we would be ready to use one of those tools, and we expect they will be sufficiently mature by that stage."

## 14.6. Timeline

"Whether we build the data centers ourselves or have someone else build them, they will be available towards mid-2013," says Kerrison. "This simply a reflection of how long it takes to construct a facility. Obviously, a collocation provider would be more immediate. Then it is probably three to five years from that stage: three years to do the bulk of the work, and then several more years to tidy up everything. It depends to a great extent on how much effort we throw at it. If we move the three existing data centers in the Netherlands sequentially, it would be nine to twelve months for each. It can be parallelized a little, but that depends on the business risk and the budget."

Kerrison is not afraid of capacity problems, possibly stalling innovation while working on this new infrastructure. "Quite the opposite. We are simplifying the infrastructure such that we can get much more done. So we will continue on our innovation on the product side, but thanks to the new infrastructure we should be able to enable much more. And that will be immediately visible."

> A data center built five years ago would have a Power Usage Effectiveness of 2.0. We will be hitting a low 1.2, which really is industry leading.

# Wuxi Builds Engine for Economic Growth

Minimizing cost and maximizing speed with cloud computing

Contribution: IBM

Customer: Wuxi Lake Tai, China

Industry: Government

Solution: cloud computing, PaaS, optimizing IT, service management

# 15. Wuxi Builds Engine for Economic Growth

Minimizing cost and maximizing speed with cloud computing

## 15.1. Executive Overview

Located in Jiangsu Province in south-eastern China, Wuxi is a major center for industry and commerce, ranked in the top fifteen cities in China. Among its other responsibilities, the municipal government must balance the need for economic development with the requirement to preserve its natural resources and safeguard the well-being of its population of more than four million people.

**Business need**

Create flexible, shared computing resources for local government projects and for software development start-ups; provide complete virtual infrastructure precisely sized for each requirement; lower barriers to market entry for new companies by eliminating need to commit capital to in-house infrastructure.
Solution
Worked with IBM to deploy the Wuxi Cloud Center, based on IBM Blue Cloud technology and featuring both x86 and IBM Power Architecture servers. The cloud hosts the full IBM Rational Suite of software development and testing tools, and will later provide other IBM software on a pay-as-you-use model.

**Benefits**

Shared infrastructure enables high utilization of available resources, delivering better cost-efficiency; each company's virtual resources can be flexed up and down as required, and priced according to usage; cloud paradigm offers almost instant set-up and total flexibility, with zero requirement for customers to own or even understand the underlying infrastructure.

## 15.2. The Wuxi Case

Located in Jiangsu Province in south-eastern China, Wuxi is a major center for industry and commerce, ranked in the top fifteen cities in China. Among its other responsibilities, the municipal government must balance the need for economic development with the requirement to preserve its natural resources and safeguard the well-being of its population of more than four million people.
When a combination of factors produced an unprecedented algal bloom in Lake Tai, the large body of fresh water on which Wuxi is situated, the municipal government embarked on an ambitious program of environmental development and relocation of industries. By shutting down or relocating heavily polluting factories and creating more environmentally friendly business parks, the government aimed not only to reverse the damage to the local eco-system but also to move towards a more sustainable, services-led economy.

With a large number of highly educated software engineers and business graduates in its population, Wuxi had the opportunity to take a leading position in both the local and international markets for software. Recognizing that start-up companies did not always have the financial capital required to invest in enterprise-class IT infrastructure, the municipal government decided to create a hi-tech business park offering shared resources on a pay-as-you-use basis. The government's aim was simultaneously to meet its own internal IT requirements in the most flexible and cost-effective manner possible.

To ensure that shared services would be available not just inside the business park but across the whole municipal area, Wuxi opted for a cloud computing solution from IBM. "We recognized that IBM is a global leader in cloud services, and we were also attracted by the company's strong presence and support network in China," said Paul Lu, CEO of Wuxi Cloud Center. The combination of the IBM Smart Business cloud portfolio and IBM Blue Cloud technology enabled Wuxi to create a flexible platform for delivering rich services via the Internet.

## 15.3.  Phase 1: Flexible Resources

In the initial phase of its cloud deployment, Wuxi created a set of shared, virtualized resources to meet the requirements of internal development teams within the municipal government. The cloud provides the full IBM Rational Suite of software development and testing tools. There are currently twelve separate government projects using the cloud, which provides securely isolated environments that can flex up and down to meet the changing demands of each project.

"A key benefit of the cloud is that the individual departments do not need to know anything about the underlying infrastructure - they simply get precisely the computing resources they need at any given time," said Paul Lu. "The solution includes services running on both Intel Xeon and POWER6 processors, but from the end-user's point of view, there's no complexity and no concerns about integration."

## 15.4.  Phase 2: Rapid, Right-Sized Deployment

In the second phase, Wuxi has opened the cloud to the 150 companies registered in the New Town Science and Education Industrial Park. The cloud effectively enables new software development businesses to gain a virtual enterprise-class data center, complete with all the Rational tools they need, sized perfectly for their requirements. Creating a new private environment for each business takes a matter of minutes - compared with the weeks or months it would take for a business to build its own physical data center and deploy its own software - so new businesses can hit the ground running.

According to Paul Lu the cloud reduces the significant barrier to entry for start-up companies in the software development businesses: "In the past, a new company would not typically have the time or the financial capital to invest in building up an enterprise-class data center. With the IBM cloud, we can rapidly deliver a secure set of virtual resources, providing all the performance and availability of a world-class data center, sized and priced to fit each company's profile."

Rather than having capital tied up in an inflexible physical infrastructure, start-up companies using the Wuxi cloud pay a variable fee according to the amount of compute resources they consume. In addition to the Rational tools, they can also use IBM WebSphere Application Server and IBM DB2 information management software. The cloud resources are managed and orchestrated using IBM Tivoli systems management software. Wuxi plans to introduce new software and services, including Lotus Domino collaborative software, CRM and eCommerce applications, enabling the delivery of a full range of software-as-a-service solutions.

## 15.5. Pre-Integrated Solutions

The Wuxi cloud is built on IBM Blue Cloud technologies, which have become the foundation for IBM CloudBurst and IBM Tivoli Service Automation Manager. CloudBurst is a family of pre-integrated service delivery platforms that include the hardware, storage, networking, virtualization and service management software to create a private cloud environment, transform data centers, and build dynamic infrastructures that deliver new levels of service at reduced cost.

## 15.6. Seeding Clouds for Growth

By transforming an industrial zone into a state-of-the-art business park offering IBM cloud computing, Wuxi has created a true engine for growth. The Wuxi cloud has the capacity to provide services to hundreds of small and mid-sized software development companies, providing powerful tools and flexible resources that help lower the barriers to market entry. Paul Lu: "The completely flexible, pay-as-you-use model allows start-ups to bring new high-quality software to market faster and without requiring large amounts of capital investment. Effectively, the IBM cloud gives each company the right-sized virtual infrastructure, ready to flex up or down as their needs change."

### Products and services used
IBM products and services that were used in this case study:

### Hardware
IBM BladeCenter chassis with a management blade and three further HS22 blades
IBM Power Systems
IBM System Storage DS3400

### Software
IBM Rational Suite
IBM DB2 for AIX
IBM WebSphere Application Server
IBM Tivoli Provisioning Manager
IBM Tivoli Monitoring
IBM Systems Director with Active Energy Manager
VMware VirtualCenter

# Aviva Unites with Online Collaboration Solution

Contribution: Microsoft
Customer: Aviva
Industry: Finance
Solution: cloud computing, SaaS, hosted service

# 16. Aviva Unites with Online Collaboration Solution

## 16.1. Executive Overview

Aviva is a global life and general insurance services company. It has offices in 28 countries with 46,000 employees serving 50 million customers.

**Business need**

In 2007 Aviva started a process to unify the company under a single brand. Global communication and collaboration across the business was a key challenge. This required both a technical environment and cultural change.

**Solution**

Aviva implemented Microsoft Office SharePoint Online as its communications environment and partnered with Microsoft Services, which deployed the solution quickly and cost-effectively within the tight 150-day timeframe.

**Benefits**

- ▷ Savings in project delivery.

- ▷ Reduced project risk: the software-plus-service model helped ensure efficient delivery, with a much lower demand on Aviva technical staff to support deployment.

- ▷ Improved cross-organization collaboration: Office SharePoint Online provided a user-centric focus, with very little training required to support the adoption by staff. It also allowed knowledge and the institutional memory to be stored, easily searched, and accessed by the right people at the right time.

- ▷ The portal has significantly improved employee productivity. Employees can build their own sites easily. Forums, blogs, and wikis help employees put forward their opinions on matters such as savings, leadership, and customer engagement—increasing debate and exchanges of ideas and information.

## 16.2. The Aviva Case

Aviva is a global life and general insurance services company. It has offices in 28 countries with 46,000 employees serving 50 million customers, and first started operating more than 300 years ago. In 2007, Chief Executive Officer Andrew Moss set out his strategic vision—One Aviva, Twice the Value—to unify the company under a single brand, worldwide.
As the fifth-largest insurance group worldwide, Aviva provides savings, investments, and insurance, and has been operating since 1696. The company serves more than 50 million people in 28 countries. Aviva is now one of the leading providers of life and pension products in Europe, with a market-leading position in the UK, and is actively expanding its business in Asia Pacific and the US. The group specializes in long-term savings, fund management, and general insurance. In 2008, Aviva generated premium income and investment sales of £51 billion (US$85 billion), and held £381 billion of funds under management.

Andrew Moss joined Aviva as Chief Finance Officer in 2004, becoming global Chief Executive Officer in July 2007. He defined a new vision for the group—One Aviva, Twice the Value—to drive the company to an even higher level of performance. This included a focus on:

- ▸ Developing the group's existing businesses.

- ▸ Creating a strong regional business unit structure.

- ▸ Rigorously allocating capital resources.

- ▸ Increasing customer reach.

- ▸ Boosting productivity.

The company needed the capacity to communicate with and engage all employees but had no platform to do so. There was no easy way to unify regional initiatives, share best practices, and ensure consistency. Aviva wanted to encourage innovation, improve efficiency, and enhance the teamwork required for continued success.

> A unified global intranet would provide a key tool for Aviva to implement cultural change internally

A unified global intranet would provide a key tool for Aviva to implement cultural change internally and develop its business strategy for the coming decades. It needed to provide market-leading collaboration capabilities for employees and also support them in gathering and accessing of knowledge on a worldwide basis. The solution—called Aviva World—was set to launch within 150 days, setting a highly demanding challenge.

## 16.3. Defining the IT Challenge

Toby Redshaw was hired as the global Chief Information Officer in the first quarter of 2008. Redshaw: "Firstly, we needed a global intranet—something that was easy to use and manage, and would help change the culture of the company. Secondly, we wanted a knowledge and collaboration environment to help people retain the institutional memory of the company, capture the knowledge that often leaves when people move on, and work in teams faster, better, and cheaper. It had to be an accessible store with first-class search capabilities." Another of Redshaw's goals was to compress the delivery cycle time in IT from concept to solution. Aviva needed this solution to reach everyone quickly and easily. The challenge was determining how to be locally present and agile, while benefiting from technology on a global scale. Accordingly, Redshaw asked Matt Fahy, Global IT Services Director at Aviva, to lead the project and deliver it in a rapid and innovative way.

Aviva began to search for a partner to implement the business solution. Fahy says: "Aviva wanted a partner that could take responsibility for the entire solution. Microsoft Services could work with us end to end for a single solution. It had deep technical expertise and the ability to manage a complex program, including multiple partners, while helping us to build an in-house center of excellence."

## 16.4. Solution

The Aviva World global solution was based on Microsoft Office SharePoint Online, which has been fully licensed for three years. It provides enterprise content management and search, including document management, Web content records, and rights management.

It also allows the creation of wikis and blogs, and enhanced business intelligence with key performance indicator dashboards.

Redshaw says: "The solution brought Aviva a communications portal, a modern collaboration environment, a knowledge platform using new tools, and a foundation for us to use as a launch pad for further applications."

In the first quarter of 2008, Aviva embraced software-plus-services, granting Microsoft preferred vendor status. Fahy says: "We chose to work with Microsoft because it offered us a great environment, and was strong in user interaction. Microsoft could offer Office SharePoint Online in a hosted environment over the Internet, and make it available very quickly."

Redshaw adds: "We looked at total cost of ownership and examined the underlying architecture, focusing on the ability to provide services with the software to ensure success. We then evaluated the roadmaps, including the two-, three-, and four-year impact. I needed to make a software decision that looked good this quarter, next quarter, next year, and the year after. We felt we were getting a solution—we were getting software and a service. This was a whole package that looked like it was more about the solution inside the company, and also about the benefit we'll provide to our business and our partners."

The first phase began in June 2008 with a deadline for delivery in late 2008. With Microsoft Services driving the project, the hosted service was delivered ahead of the challenging 150-day target. Redshaw says: "Together with Microsoft, we hit the overall goal in 142 days and helped Aviva achieve the deployment in around one half of the cost of the original budget. However, while appreciating the savings, we're most excited about the functionality Microsoft Online Services is bringing to Aviva."

## 16.5. Benefits

Office SharePoint Online offered a user-friendly global social intranet, which has vastly improved collaboration across the organization. Under the leadership of Microsoft Services, a number of Microsoft partners acted as a unified team to ensure that targets were met in a cost-effective way. Aviva has achieved savings in project delivery and has developed a strategic business tool that will provide opportunity for further implementation of Microsoft technology.

### Reduced Project Risk

The software-plus-service model helped ensure efficient delivery, with a much lower demand on Aviva technical staff to support deployment. But critical to the success of the project was pulling together the various elements of the project, with different partners leading different work streams.

Microsoft Services took the lead role as solution partner, while working closely with a number of key partner organizations, including Accenture, Avanade, and Oxford Consulting Associates. After six weeks spent defining the project scope, Microsoft Services delivered the project under fixed price terms, reducing risk for Aviva. Following a successful conclusion of the first phase of the project, Microsoft Services is continuing to provide Aviva with development expertise, using Microsoft Global Services India offshore resources for cost-effective delivery, while also providing on-going support for the solution.

### Improved Cross-Organization Collaboration

Keeping Aviva teams locally agile, while benefiting from content on a global scale, requires technology to be easy to use and manage. Office SharePoint Online helped Aviva to provide a user-centric focus, with very little training required to support the adoption by staff. It also allowed knowledge and the institutional memory to be stored, easily searched, and accessed by the right people at the right time.

The portal has significantly improved employee productivity and collaboration across the organization. Employees can build their own sites easily. Forums, blogs, and wikis help employees put forward their opinions on matters such as savings, leadership, and customer engagement—increasing debate and exchanges of ideas and information.

The first stage of the adoption of Aviva World was driven by the use of forums, team sites, and key content. Office SharePoint Online provides a collaboration platform, but it is the information architecture and site design that ensures people can find what they need, where they expect to find it.

Microsoft Services was able to create a structure that allowed better information sharing in a consistent manner between different groups within Aviva. Microsoft Services also advised Aviva on how to ensure the right content was transferred to the portal, and done so in a way that could take advantage of the full search capabilities of Office SharePoint Online.

Fahy says: "Recently, Aviva held a 24-hour online session—using the Aviva World intranet—with all its businesses across the world. The event marked a milestone in our move to a global brand, and we wanted to celebrate the future of the organization. This type of global event would never have been possible without Microsoft portal technology. A year ago, we couldn't imagine hosting a 24-hour global event."

## Fast Implementation and Savings

"Our new communications portal is less expensive than other solutions we were considering," Fahy says. "There are things we've done since the rollout that have been more cost-effective than if we had not gone down this path."

For example, Aviva recently needed to build a human resources (HR) feedback tool for employees and managers. Fahy says: "HR budgeted a significant sum to develop and host this tool based on a third-party provider proposal, but the Aviva IT team built this internally using Office SharePoint Online for one tenth of the cost anticipated."

## 16.6. Increased Integration

Redshaw is dedicated to continuing to transform Aviva. He says: "Our IT department is making a three to four year investment, analysing underlying architecture and engineering skills required to support it. The longer term roadmap includes increased integration with other Microsoft products, with future plans to deploy Microsoft Office Communications Server 2007."

Redshaw summarises: "This Microsoft environment has transformed the company in an amazingly tight window. Microsoft helped us deliver faster, with lower risk, and more cost-effectively than if we'd tried to do it ourselves. This is the beginning of the journey and we're really excited about 2010 and beyond."

# City of Zwolle Virtualizes its Desktop Systems

Customer: City of Zwolle

Industry: Government

Solution: flexible workplaces, thin clients, virtual desktop interface, streamed applications, centralized office productivity infrastructure.

# 17. City of Zwolle Virtualizes its Desktop Systems

## 17.1. Executive Overview

The city of Zwolle is the capital of the Dutch province of Overijssel. It is situated between four rivers and has almost 120,000 citizens. Over the last two years, the municipality has reorganized its desktop systems. Today, 1100 workplaces in all have been virtualized.

**Business need**

Zwolle had about 1500 workplaces for 1250 civil servants, spread over thirty locations. The complexity of the environment, the diversity of the hardware, and the decentralized setup made this infrastructure expensive to maintain. Moreover, energy costs were too high and login times were far too long, the latter resulting in a bad user experience.

**Solution**

In a European tender procedure, Pecoma was selected from five IT service providers to virtualize the municipality's workplaces. Wherever possible, desktop systems were replaced by thin clients. The new infrastructure is based on VMware Infrastructure, VMware View, and Wyse thin clients.

**Benefits**

The centralized office productivity infrastructure allows users to connect to their virtualized workplace from any device, at any time or place. The login time has been reduced to one minute. At this moment, no reliable measurements of the energy consumption can be made, so it is unclear whether the projected energy savings have been realized. If all goes according to plan, the systems management department will be reduced from thirteen to twelve FTEs (full-time equivalents).

## 17.2. Main Goal: Reducing Energy Consumption

The Zwolle has virtualized its workplaces. Using thin clients and a Virtual Desktop Infrastructure (VDI), Zwolle aimed to improve flexibility and user experience as well as reduce complexity, maintenance costs and energy consumption.
During the last two years, the municipal government has been reorganizing its desktop systems. Today, 1100 workplaces in all have been virtualized. "Zwolle maintained about 1500 workplaces for 1250 civil servants, spread over thirty locations in the city," says Jaap van Vliet, until recently in the unit Advice and Facilities responsible for the information delivery in the organization. "These are replaced by 1100 thin clients. About 150 workstations will not be virtualized, such, for example, as those used for heavy graphics applications."

### Green City

Saving energy was the most important aim of this transition. Two years ago, the city had IT service provider Pecoma perform an energy optimization scan. It found that energy usage of the IT environment could be reduced by almost fifty percent. To realize these savings, the fat

Windows desktops at the front-end would be replaced by Wyse thin clients, in combination with energy-saving monitors. These are then fed by operating system images running on a virtualized server infrastructure. This allows hardware resources to be automatically brought offline when not in use.

Another aim was to improve the service to the end user. Specifically, login times were far too long. For this reason, measuring the quality of the services provided was an important part of this transition. "We consider the end users to be our customers, and we want to provide them with a good service," says Van Vliet.

### More Management Needed

Nearing the completion of this project, Van Vliet has learned that a virtualized environment requires increased management. "If a Windows desktop system crashes, it can simply be rebooted. When Windows-applications fail in a VDI-environment, sessions and connections get stuck. That means we have to monitor and guide our users more intensively."

Since applications are now being streamed to the users, it needs to be explained to them why that takes more time. "Logging in has become a lot faster. But then users say 'gee, I thought everything would be lightning fast now'. Currently, we are working on the performance of the applications. Packaging these in a way that the software keeps performing well is an art in itself. The login should be completed within one minute."

That milestone has been reached now. "Eventually, we want to get this down to thirty seconds. And ultimately an application should start up within seven to twenty seconds. We are continuing to measure this," Van Vliet explains.

"The streamed applications are performing really well," Pecoma's Business Manager Arjen Visser elaborates. "There is hardly any difference compared to locally installed software, except for heavy applications like Autodesk 3ds Max."

To explain the changes to the users, flyers describing the new setup were distributed within the organization, supplemented by extensive additional information on the intranet.

## 17.3. Specials

Not all fat clients at the city of Zwolle will be replaced. The exceptions are denoted as 'specials'. "There are always groups of systems and applications that cannot be virtualized that easily," says Sebo Noorda, Portfolio Manager at Pecoma. AutoCAD is the most common example. "However, the starting point of course remains to move everything to the back-end." For heavier applications, blade PCs could be deployed. In this case, Zwolle chose otherwise because of cost considerations. That means that they will have to put in extra effort maintaining this hybrid environment. "We regularly check whether the remaining applications can be virtualized," Visser adds. "If that proves to work out for a certain package, we transfer the users to the virtualized environment."

The image holding the operating system is kept as clean as possible. The applications are delivered to the users using streaming technology. During the last year, Pecoma had three or four people on site creating the software packages. They did that together with the application managers, so the latter will be able to take care of this themselves in the future. Furthermore, this saved some costs. As a consequence, competences of the IT managers have shifted. "Application managers had to learn how to build ThinApp/MSI packages," says Visser, "while the workload for the Windows managers has been reduced. Currently, the number of FTEs is still the same, but that may change in the future."

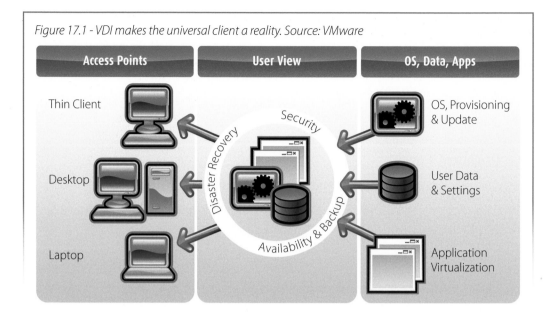

Figure 17.1 - VDI makes the universal client a reality. Source: VMware

**Access Points** — **User View** — **OS, Data, Apps**

Thin Client

Desktop

Laptop

Security

Disaster Recovery

Availability & Backup

OS, Provisioning & Update

User Data & Settings

Application Virtualization

### Application Packaging

As with the systems, not all applications will be virtualized. "Software used by everybody, like Microsoft Office, is delivered as part of the image," says Noorda. "Often these applications have a lot of connections to other software and to the operating system," Visser adds. "Office being the most notable example."

Then there are applications that are hard to capture in a package, for example because they use specific hardware drivers. "That is why you need to consider maintenance issues at the start of a project like this," Noorda explains. "If you put applications into the image too easily now, it may catch up with you later."

> The "laptop problem": "Especially at higher management levels people are strongly attached to their independence."

Zwolle has been able to bring the number of applications from 350 down to 300, from which a little more than half have been packaged. Noorda expects about fifteen percent of these to end up in the operating system image. "The image contains all applications that could not be packaged or were not performing well. Currently there are about twenty of these," he says. Over the years this number is expected to go down. "Microsoft and VMware are constantly introducing new technologies allowing more and more applications to be virtualized."

### Thin Laptops?

The original plan to replace notebooks at the same time had to be mothballed. Only a few people handed in theirs after finding a thin client better suited to their needs. Thin laptops are a fairly new technology. The offline desktop does not work properly in the current version. So Zwolle is marking time here. But eventually, Wyse's thin laptops will be deployed as well.

"We wanted people to work from their own desktop when at home, and from a thin laptop when on the road," Van Vliet says, "But we decided to allow the notebooks for the time being. From a rational point of view, you only need a laptop if you are out a lot and actually working on the road. Working at home can be supported by other means. But there is also a cultural component. Especially at higher management levels people are strongly attached to their independence. We have to acknowledge that. Later on, the transition of the laptops will be a separate project."

"Mistakes are often the best teachers," Van Vliet emphasizes. "The project also took longer than we expected. That was caused by some technical problems we had with the software. Through Pecoma, we had VMware implement some bug fixes. The deployment could only continue after solving these issues." This was one of the reasons the transition took about half a year longer than planned.

The same goes for the budget; it was exceeded at several points. According to Visser, the costs for the extension of the Storage Area Network (SAN) were estimated too low. The packaging and testing of the software applications required extra consulting capacity. And additional investments were needed for licenseslicences and adjustments to the server room.

## 17.4. Limited Results

At this moment, it is not clear whether the projected savings in energy will be realized. "We are not yet able to take good measurements," says Visser. "Furthermore, the Zwolle data center now also hosts a backup environment for the province of Overijssel, requiring a considerable amount of energy. So it is hard to come up with reliable numbers."

Despite the virtualized environment requiring more management, Van Vliet still sees opportunities for savings here, one of the initial goals of the project. "We see a shift in management activities to Windows management. Furthermore, Windows and application managers are now working together more closely. I can see savings in the future. We think we can eventually cancel out one FTE (of thirteen)."

At this moment, Zwolle is preparing a backup facility at the data center of the province of Overijssel. Possibly part of the VDI environment can be moved there as well. In the near future, Zwolle is considering upgrading to Windows 7. But there are not yet any concrete plans. Vista will not be deployed.

## Virtualized Infrastructure

The central virtualized infrastructure is based on VMware View. Storage has already been centralized. So the new Virtual Desktop Infrastructure (VDI) can join in with the existing IT resources.

The back-end of the virtualized desktops, consisting of 750 to 800 concurrent sessions, runs on twelve IBM x3850 servers, each featuring four processors and 128 gigabytes of internal memory. This way, each system can execute up to a hundred virtualized desktops.

The existing SAN system (Storage Area Network), an IBM DS8100 storage array, has been extended with new disk enclosures, enough to host the desktop images and sessions. Furthermore, this upgrade also improves the performance and the user experience.

To make sure users have enough bandwidth at their hands to also play multimedia without any problems, each virtualization server comes with four four-way Ethernet adapters. In the near future, PC-over-IP will be deployed to further exploit the available bandwidth. The new operating system image is now ready and waiting to be distributed.

# Evolution of the Internal Compute Cloud at Washington Mutual

Contribution: VMware
Customer: Washington Mutual
Industry: Banking
Solution: virtualization, cloud computing

# 18. Evolution of the Internal Compute Cloud at Washington Mutual

## 18.1. Executive Overview

The Washington Mutual (WaMu) bank, now a division of JPMorgan Chase, started its move to an internal compute fabric three years ago.

**Business need**

Their business goals included lowering IT deployment and operational costs and obtaining a predictable and faster application model. They also wanted to increase the flexibility, agility, and scalability of the IT environment. The biggest demand of the internal customers was the ability to make changes to their compute environment without having to make dramatic changes to the physical infrastructure. WaMu also wanted to improve server utilization across the enterprise.

**Solution**

Washington Mutual moved to cloud computing over a three-year period. They first moved to permanent allocations of virtual servers. In phase 2 they shifted to transient allocations of virtual servers. In the final phase WaMu targeted allocations of compute on demand – self-service-based, highly automated deployments of user-defined and user-funded periods of compute time.

**Benefits**

As a result of moving to the cloud computing model utilizing the VMware solution, WaMu has realized the following benefits:

- Virtual server footprint has grown to >1,500 servers.

- Utility compute is typically 40-70 percent more cost effective than equivalent physical servers.

- Unit costs for individual VMs have fallen 60 percent in 18 months.

- Deployment times for a virtual server are now less than five days.

- The cloud/utility program is fully self-funded and continues to grow.

## 18.2. The Washington Mutual Case

Washington Mutual (WaMu), now a division of JPMorgan Chase, started its move to an internal compute fabric three years ago. "Our business goals included lowering IT deployment and operational costs and obtaining a predictable and faster application model," stated Barton Warner, first VP and senior group manager and enterprise architect. "We also wanted to increase infrastructure flexibility, agility, and scalability to be able to respond to business needs quickly. The biggest demand from our internal customer base was the ability to make changes to their compute environment and the underlying cost structure without having to make dramatic and fundamental forklift changes to the physical infrastructure."

WaMu also wanted to improve server utilization across the enterprise. "Our average utilization was running at an average of 10 percent on about 9,000 distributed servers. We needed to drive that number up significantly. We also wanted to develop a faster deployment mode. Deployment times were typically in the 60-70 day range for any new physical asset from ordering to operational status." Working with VMware from the beginning, WaMu's move to cloud computing progressed in four distinct phases over a three-year period:

- ▢ Islands of compute: WaMu started in 2006 with 9,000 traditional, physical server deployments. This model was inflexible, underutilized and costly.

- ▢ Compute pools: WaMu then moved to permanent allocations of virtual servers. This resulted in more flexibility, better utilization and cost-effectiveness. But the company still had many virtual servers sitting idle and needed to plan for peak loads.

- ▢ Dynamic compute: WaMu then shifted its focus to transient allocations of virtual servers. This created a highly flexible and highly cost-effective environment. Virtual machines were requested and allocated in 30-day increments. But there were still virtual servers sitting idle, and teams didn't always need the compute for as long as a full month.

- ▢ On-demand compute: In the final phase of its move to cloud computing, WaMu targeted allocations of compute on demand – self-service-based, highly automated deployments of user-defined and user-funded periods of compute time.

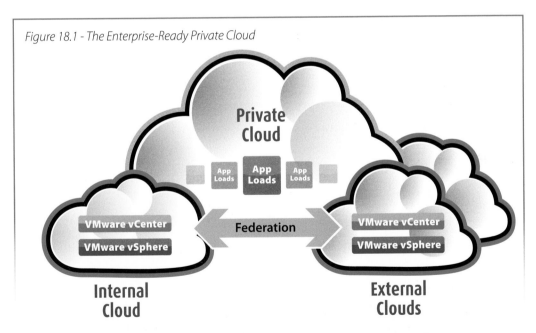

*Figure 18.1 - The Enterprise-Ready Private Cloud*

WaMu's cloud computing program has dramatically reduced waste and complexity from its IT environment by allowing hardware and software to be leveraged more efficiently across the enterprise. Utility computing is now delivering scalable and on-demand computing platforms through the use of standardized building blocks coupled with the ability to allocate and provision services on-demand. Rationalization and simplification of WaMu's infrastructure is reducing IT costs through elimination of redundant technologies – not just limited to hardware, but including all software, information and business services.

As a result of moving to the cloud computing model utilizing the VMware solution, WaMu has realized the following benefits:

- Virtual server footprint has grown to >1,500 servers.

- Utility compute is typically 40-70 percent more cost effective than equivalent physical servers.

- Unit costs for individual VMs have fallen 60 percent in 18 months.

- Deployment times for a virtual server are now less than five days.

- The cloud/utility program is fully self-funded and continues to grow.

## 18.3. Recommendations

When asked what advice he could give to other enterprises considering the move to a cloud computing environment, Warner recommended the following steps:

### Step 1. Standardize and Simplify All Offerings

- Focus on building a repeatable set of building blocks.

- Target adoption for 80 percent of deployments.

- Develop easy to understand costing metrics.

### Step 2. Use Server Consolidation to Drive Critical Mass

- Use virtualization to consolidate workloads.

- Refresh all aging systems onto virtual platforms.

- Build trust with application development teams and business process owners.

### Step 3. Automate and Refine the Offerings

- Deploy tools to drive transparency for platform users.

- Automate the deployment and lifecycle processes.

- Actively seek customer feedback and develop an advisory group to promote adoption.

"The difference between utility and cloud-based computing is that the enterprise cloud really focuses on true, on-demand computing"

"I see the difference between utility and cloud-based computing is that the enterprise cloud really focuses on true, on-demand compute," explained Warner. "When somebody needs it, they get it. And if they need it for one day, they get it for just one day. Then they have the tools to destroy that workload at the end of the day or suspend it to disk, based on individual business parameters so they can provide that compute exactly when needed.

That's the most efficient model. And for WaMu, whether I do that within the four walls of my data center, or whether I use a third-party partner to do that is what cloud is all about. In the financial services industry, I see companies starting to focus on this model internally first – leveraging multiple data centers and looking at how cloud enables the taking and using of excess capacity – but over time, this notion of a federated cloud is really quite viable because it enables this true on-demand footprint."

# City of San Antonio (Texas) Consolidates Servers and Delivers Application Services

Contribution: Oracle/Sun

Subject: virtualization, server consolidation

Industry: Government

# 19. City of San Antonio Consolidates Servers and Delivers Application Services

## 19.1. Executive Overview

Residents of the City of San Antonio (CoSA) go online to pay a traffic ticket, apply for a job, or find information about the dozens of activities that affect their community. CoSA employees rely on their IT-systems to get access to applications and data used in daily work activities, including financial systems, human resources software, and public safety applications used by the police and fire departments. Over the years, the City's server infrastructure had sprawled to keep pace with its service delivery, and CoSA was running out of room in its datacenter.

### Business need

The City of San Antonio wanted to reduce datacenter costs, simplify management, ensure availability of services and provide room for future growth.

### Solution

To streamline management, the City of San Antonio replaced approximately 115 legacy servers with 26 Sun servers. It used virtualization technology to consolidate servers and ensure the availability of mission-critical applications.

### Benefits

Due to the server consolidation energy consumption was cut by more than 15% and server footprint was reduced by over 85%. The performance and reliability of the new IT-infrastructure has improved. Employees gained more time for projects that enhance service delivery and availability. CoSA expects to realize a full ROI within two and a half years based on reduced support costs alone.

## 19.2. The San Antonio Case

Residents of the City of San Antonio (CoSA) go online to pay a traffic ticket, apply for a job, or find information about the dozens of activities that affect their community. CoSA employees rely on their IT-systems to get access to applications and data used in daily work activities, including financial systems, human resources software, and public safety applications used by the police and fire departments.

Over the years, the City's server infrastructure had sprawled to keep pace with its service delivery, and CoSA was running out of room in its datacenter. The City's Information Technology Services Department (ITSD) needed to develop a plan to upgrade its IT infrastructure to reduce maintenance costs and enhance service. It planned to replace dozens of under-utilized servers with fewer higher performance systems, and it also decided to implement a second datacenter to ensure business continuity.

In mid-2008, CoSA considered several options for datacenter optimization. The City had a long relationship with Sun, using many of its legacy servers to run mission-critical Oracle databases and SAP applications. In the end, it felt that leveraging Sun's SPARC servers as a platform for the Solaris 10 Operating System and Solaris Zones provided the best roadmap for return on investment (ROI) with its virtualization technologies and energy-efficient, mainframe-class servers. Lumenate — a Texas-based technical consulting firm and systems reseller — also provided valuable insight into designing a virtual environment optimized for SAP applications.

## 19.3. Consolidation

The City manages several separate environments, including one based on SAP and Oracle solutions, and another with applications and core services running on Windows. CoSA decided to consolidate its SAP NetWeaver systems and Oracle database applications on Sun SPARC servers.

CoSA also migrated from the Solaris 9 to the Solaris 10 Operating System to take advantage of Solaris Zones, so multiple applications can run in isolation from one another on the same physical hardware. The solution also includes Sun Blade 6000 Modular Systems, and multiple Sun Fire T2000 servers. CoSA also replaced 80 physical Windows servers with 12 Sun Fire servers as a VMWare virtual infrastructure platform in its Windows environment. Altogether, the City consolidated or replaced approximately 115 servers with 26 energy-efficient servers from Sun.

CoSA believes that the speed and high throughput of the servers running on the Solaris 10 OS is the ideal combination for running its SAP and Oracle systems. "We're very happy with our solution," says Cathryn Major, administrator on the City of San Antonio UNIX team. "If our database administrators have a choice, they want an Oracle database and they want it to run on Sun technology."

By using Sun servers and virtualization technology, CoSA has consolidated from 16 to 4 racks of servers and reduced the datacenter footprint for these workloads by over 85%.

This footprint is distributed across two geographically diverse datacenters to ensure business continuity.

> Although it has dramatically increased its server infrastructure capacity by implementing virtualization technology and higher performing hardware, CoSA has also reduced maintenance overhead.

Although it has dramatically increased its server infrastructure capacity by implementing virtualization technology and higher performing hardware, CoSA has also reduced maintenance overhead. Administrators now have more time available for deploying new systems that benefit the City. Major points out it could previously take a week or more to deploy a physical server, but now it takes half an hour to set up a Solaris Zone. "We've been able to set up a lot more projects for people by using Sun's virtualization technology," she says. The efficiencies gained from the server modernization effort extend beyond the boundaries of the IT organization. Since the City deployed SAP's ERP suite in 2004, application response times had been steadily increasing to the extent that the user experience was negatively impacted and productivity was beginning to suffer. Once the SAP application and database workloads were redistributed across the M4000 and M5000 servers, the City immediately realized a nearly three-fold performance improvement, and the SAP system response time fell well below the threshold of negatively impacting end-user effectiveness. This translates into increased productivity and a higher ROI for the City's SAP solution.

## 19.4. Cost Savings

But consolidation has affected more than productivity - the City has realized considerable cost savings as well. CoSA expects to realize a full ROI within two and a half years based on reduced support costs alone. It has also dropped its overall datacenter energy consumption by approximately 15% by using fewer and more energy-efficient systems while increasing workload count by over 30%. Most importantly, CoSA has gained control of its server infrastructure while continuing to grow services for the people of San Antonio.

> The overall datacenter energy consumption has dropped by approximately 15% by using fewer and more energy-efficient systems while increasing workload count by over 30%.

The City of San Antonio (CoSA) wanted to cut energy consumption and streamline management. For example, it ran over 300 under-utilized physical Windows servers to support core services, departmental applications, databases, and web servers on the Microsoft Windows platform. "We wanted to reduce the amount of hardware, support costs, and maintenance downtimes," says Rick Barnds, manager of the City of San Antonio Windows infrastructure team. "We also wanted to consolidate workloads."

To consolidate, CoSA opted to accelerate its server virtualization strategy by replacing 80 of the Windows servers with six Sun Fire X4600 M2 servers with VMware ESXi virtualization technology. It also deployed six additional Sun Fire servers to support over 30 new critical public safety application workloads in an N+1 configuration. "We chose the Sun Fire X4600 servers because we needed a system that could accommodate multiple processors and large amounts of memory," says Barnds. "The servers have a very high I/O capability ideal for handling a lot of workloads. We also wanted hardware that was going to be stable and well-constructed - we wanted enterprise-class hardware." By deploying mission-critical resources such as a fuel management system and public safety applications, CoSA has improved service availability and met its administration goals as well. The reliability of the new servers combined with virtualization technology also helps CoSA keep critical services online. Barnds: "If we have any kind of emergency with a server, we can stand up another one in a matter of minutes and we're back in business."

# Sources

- Carr Nicholas G, *'Does IT Matter?'*, Harvard Business Press, May 2003
- Cisco, *'Cloud: Powered by the Network - What a Business Leader Must Know'*, White Paper, 2010
- Cloud Security Alliance, *'Top Threats to Cloud Computing V1.0'*, March 2010
- Desisto Robert P. *'Four Steps to Get in Front of the SaaS Curve'*, Gartner, June 2010
- EMC Consulting, *'Private Cloud Means Business: Costs Down and Agility Up'*, 2010
- EMC, *'EMC's IT's Journey to the Private Cloud: A Practioner's Guide'*, July 2010
- ESG, *'IT Audit - EMC's Journey to the Private Cloud'*, May 2010
- Forrester Consulting (Stefan Ried, Ph.D., Holger Kisker, Ph.D., and Pascal Matzke), *'The Evolution Of Cloud Computing Markets'*, July 6, 2010
- Forrester Consulting, *'The Business Value Of Virtualization'*, July 2009
- Gartner, *'Dataquest Insight: Virtualization Market Size Driven by Cost Reduction, Resource Utilization and Management Advantages'*, January 2009
- Hurwitz Judith, Robin Bloor, Marcia Kaufman, *'Cloud Computing for Dummies'*, Wiley Publishing, 2010, HP Edition
- IBM, *'Defining a Framework for Cloud Adoption'*, White Paper May 2020
- IBM, *'The Benefits of Cloud Computing'*, July 2009
- IDC Executive Brief, *'Cloud Computing in the Midmarket: Assessing the Options'*, August 2010
- Jahn Keith, *'Making the Cloud Relevant: e-business, IT as a Service, and Everything as a Service'*, April 2010
- Mayo Richard, Perng Charles, *'Cloud Computing Payback, An explanation of where the ROI comes from'*, IBM, November 2009
- Mell Peter, Tim Grance, *'Effectively and Securely Using the Cloud Computing Paradigm'*, Presentation NIST, July 2009
- Microsoft, *'Aviva Unites Its Global Organization Using Online Collaboration Solution'*, Case Story, February 2010
- Microsoft, *'Datacenter Management and Virtualization'*, June 2010
- Oracle, *'City Government Consolidates Servers and Delivers Enterprise Application Services with Sun Virtualization Technology'*, October 2009
- Pescatore John, *'Securing and Managing Private and Public Cloud Computing'*, Gartner, September 2010
- Scheffy Clark, *'Virtualization for Dummies'*, Wiley Publishing, 2007, AMD Edition
- Smith David Mitchell, Daryl C. Plummer, David W. Cearley, *'The What, Why and When of Cloud Computing'*, Gartner, June 2009
- T-Systems, *'Cloud Computing. Alternative sourcing strategy for business ICT'*, White Paper, no date
- T-Systems, *'Security in the cloud'*, White Paper', White Paper, no date
- VMware, *'Eight Key Ingredients for Building an Internal Cloud'*, White Paper, 2009
- VMware, *'Understanding Full Virtualization, Paravirtualization, and Hardware Assist'*, White Paper, 2007

# Relevant links

| Organization | Link |
|---|---|
| Amazon Web Services | http://aws.amazon.com/ |
| CA | www.ca.com/us/lpg/global201008/Cloud-is-the-Answer.aspx |
| Cisco Systems | www.cisco.com/en/US/netsol/ns976/index.html |
| Cloud Security Alliance | www.cloudsecurityalliance.org/ |
| The Economist | www.economist.com/node/14637206?story_id=14637206 |
| EMC | www.emc.com/leadership/programs/cloud_computing.htm |
| HP | www.hp.com/go/cloud |
| IBM | www.ibm.com/ibm/cloud/ |
| Microsoft | www.microsoft.com/cloud/ |
| NIST | csrc.nist.gov/groups/SNS/cloud-computing/ |
| Open Cloud Consortium | opencloudconsortium.org/ |
| Open Data Center Alliance | www.opendatacenteralliance.org/ |
| Oracle | www.oracle.com/us/technologies/cloud/index.htm |
| T-Systems | www.t-systems.com/tsi/en/630016/Home/Solutions/Cloud-Computing-Series |
| VMware | www.vmware.com/solutions/cloud-computing/ |
| VRC | www.virtualrealitycheck.netw |
| Wikipedia | http://en.wikipedia.org/wiki/Cloud_computing%22 |

# Glossary

| Terms | Explanation |
|-------|-------------|
| 1-to-many | One provider serves many customers. |
| Application Service Provision | Offering an application (e.g. an ERP system) over a public network (such as the Internet) or a private data network. |
| Automated Workloads | The ability to automate the management of complex workloads by using a dynamic scheduler and automation engine |
| Automatic Deprovisioning | The ability to automatically de-allocate (remove) virtual server environments as and when no longer needed, thus releasing capacity to other tasks. |
| Automatic Provisioning | The ability to automate building up virtual server environments as and when needed. |
| BRIC | Brazil, Russia, India and China. |
| Business continuity | Refers to strategies, plans and activities designed to keep ICT resource management operational. It includes scenario planning, quota management (resources) and disaster and crisis management, including resumption of regular business operations (disaster recovery). |
| Business impact | Business impact refers to the consequences and effects of an error / incident on business operations and the organization as a whole. |
| CAPEX | Capital expenditures: a capital expenditure is incurred when a business spends money either to buy fixed assets or to add to the value of an existing fixed asset with a useful life that extends beyond the taxable year: e.g. equipment, property, or industrial buildings. |
| CIO | Chief Information Officer |
| Cloud Computing | Cloud computing is a model for enabling convenient, on-demand network access to a shared pool of configurable computing resources (e.g., networks, servers, storage, applications, and services) that can be rapidly provisioned and released with minimal management effort or service provider interaction. (NIST definition). |
| Community Cloud | The cloud infrastructure is shared by several organizations and supports a specific community that has shared concerns (e.g., mission, security requirements, policy, and compliance considerations). It may be managed by the organizations or a third party and may exist on premise or off premise. |
| CRM | Customer Relationship Management (CRM) describes the procedure and technologies with which the relationship between the customer and supplier can be mapped. |
| Customizing | Customer-specific adjustments to a product or service. |

| Desktop Virtualization | Replacing the physical desktop environment with a virtual desktop hosted on a centrally located server. |
|---|---|
| Disaster recovery | The ability to resume business operations or, ideally, to maintain them without interruption after an adverse event or a disaster (earthquake, terrorist attack, etc.). |
| Due diligence | In this context, the examination of a cloud provider's reliability. It covers factors such as the provider's reputation as well as its profits and financial statements |
| Dynamic Resource Allocation | The process of automatically ensuring each virtual machine has the resources it needs as and when necessary. |
| E-collaboration | Electronically/digitally supported collaboration. |
| Elasticity | The ability to meet the needs and preferences of a non-fixed amount of users on a near real-time basis. |
| End-2-End SLA | Central management of a product or solution-orientated process from beginning to end by a service provider according to predefined service conditions. |
| ERP | Enterprise Resource Planning (ERP) denotes the business task of using the resources available in a company (capital, equipment or staff etc.) efficiently for the operational process. |
| Fat Client | A full blown PC, fully equipped for standalone or networked operation. The inexpensive alternative is a thin client, which only supports user interactions (input/output) and which use computing resources or entire applications from the network. |
| Grid computing | Form of distributed computing in which a "virtual supercomputer" is created from a cluster of loosely coupled computers. |
| Hardware token | Hardware tokens are items such as USB flash drives and smart cards with microprocessors used instead of, or in addition to, passwords or PINs in order to securely identify users in ICT systems. |
| HRM | Human Resource Management. |
| Hybrid Cloud | NIST: The cloud infrastructure is a composition of two or more clouds (private, community, or public) that remain unique entities but are bound together by standardized or proprietary technology that enables data and application portability (e.g., cloud bursting for load-balancing between clouds). |
| IaaS | NIST: The capability provided to the consumer is to provision processing, storage, networks, and other fundamental computing resources where the consumer is able to deploy and run arbitrary software, which can include operating systems and applications. The consumer does not manage or control the underlying cloud infrastructure but has control over operating systems, storage, deployed applications, and possibly limited control of select networking components (e.g., host firewalls). |
| ICT | Information and Communication Technology |

| ICT environment | An umbrella term for all computer and communications hardware and software that supports all ICT-based tasks and processes in an organization. |
|---|---|
| Incident management | Management involving fixing service malfunctions and handling service requests. |
| IT | Information Technology |
| Legacy system | An established, historically developed system |
| Multi-tenancy | a single instance of software, and the computer platform it runs on, serves multiple clients from different companies. |
| Migration | In this context, migration refers to transferring business processes to the cloud |
| NIST | National Institute of Standards and Technology (USA) |
| OPEX | An operating expense or expenditure is an ongoing cost for running a product, business or system. |
| Outsourcing | Subcontracting company tasks and structures to a third-party company. |
| Outtasking | Subcontracting individual tasks to a third-party company while the company or main contractor maintains process control. |
| Private Cloud | The cloud infrastructure is operated solely for an organization. It may be managed by the organization or a third party and may exist on premise or off premise. (NIST definition) |
| Public Cloud | The cloud infrastructure is made available to the general public or a large industry group and is owned by an organization selling cloud services. (NIST definition) |
| Recovery Strategy | Strategy of reconstructing lost data |
| Roadmap | A roadmap is a plan that describes the way forward. In this context, a roadmap lays out the steps for successfully migrating to the cloud |
| PaaS | Platform as a Service. NIST definition: The capability provided to the consumer is to deploy onto the cloud infrastructure consumer-created or acquired applications created using programming languages and tools supported by the provider. The consumer does not manage or control the underlying cloud infrastructure including network, servers, operating systems, or storage, but has control over the deployed applications and possibly application hosting environment configurations. |
| SAN | Storage Area Network |

| | |
|---|---|
| SaaS | Software as a Service. NIST definition: The capability provided to the consumer is to use the provider's applications running on a cloud infrastructure. The applications are accessible from various client devices through a thin client interface such as a web browser (e.g., web-based email). The consumer does not manage or control the underlying cloud infrastructure including network, servers, operating systems, storage, or even individual application capabilities, with the possible exception of limited user-specific application configuration settings. |
| SBC | Server Based Computing |
| Scalability | Flexible and exact adaptation of a hardware/software solution to customer needs. |
| Server Virtualization | The execution of multiple virtual server environments on one or more physical servers. |
| (SLA | A Service Level Agreement (SLA) is a formally agreed document, which is part of an ICT service agreement. It specifies measurement categories, which are regularly calculated for service inspections |
| TCO | Total Cost of Ownership (TCO) is a cost/calculation procedure and is used to help consumers and companies to estimate all costs incurred from capital goods (software, hardware etc.) |
| Thin client | User device which only support user interactions (input / output) and which use computing resources or entire applications from the network. Cheap and secure alternatives for full blown pc's (fat clients). |
| Utility Computing | Technologies and business models, with which a service provider can provide IT services on demand for its customers, billing for usage of these services. |
| VDI | Virtual Desktop Infrastructure |
| VLAN | A virtual local area network (VLAN) is a group of hosts with a common set of requirements that communicate as if they were attached to the same broadcast domain, regardless of their physical location. A VLAN has the same attributes as a physical LAN, but it allows for end stations to be grouped virtually together even if they are not located on the same network switch. |
| VPN | Virtual Private Network (VPN) denotes a computer network, whose private data – most often encrypted – is transported over a public network (e.g., the Internet). |
| Web server | A computer, which transmits documents to clients such as web browsers. |